AF614475

A LIFETIME OF MEMORIES

THE LIFE OF ELSIE EVANS

BY

ELSIE EVANS

Sarasota, Florida

ISBN: 0-9778525-7-1
Printed in the U.S.A.
Printed June, 2006

A Lifetime of Memories

Always remember to forget
The things that made you sad,
But never forget to remember
The things that made you glad.
Always remember to forget
The friends that proved untrue,
But never forget to remember
Those that have stuck by you.
Always remember to forget
The troubles that passed away,
But never forget to remember
The blessings that come each day.
– Copied –

"I thank my God upon every remembrance of you."

Thanks to everyone that has made these memories for us:
Our children,
Our 14 grandchildren,
Our 14 great-grandchildren,

Our childhood families,
And
So many, many friends

Elsie Evans

CONTENTS

THE CARNIVAL

Two little boys were sitting on the steps, trying to out-do each other as to who could remember back the farthest. One said he could remember when he was two when he went fishing with his dad. The other said, "I remember the night I was born. My Mom went to a Missionary meeting, and Grandma stayed with me."

Now, I can't remember that far back, but Mom told me she went to a carnival the night I was born. She later told me I had been on the go ever since. I just had a thought – do you suppose she got me at the carnival?

Dad and Mom got married on June 17, 1920. Dad became 17 on the 29th, and Mom turned 18 on September 3. That same year in November, they had their first child, a son, Gilbert, and eleven months later, another son, Ray. They lived in an apartment on Park Avenue in Bloomington (sounds ritzy, but it was just a short street) and then moved to the Old Franzman brick house on Unionville Road just before the bridge, which is no longer there.

From there, they moved to the little white house that still sits on the southwest corner of 10th and Dunn Streets in Bloomington, where I was born on October 12, 1923. Between

Dunn Street and Indiana Avenue on 10th, there was an alley where a house and barn sat on the east side. Dad was getting more horses and equipment for his excavating, so we moved to that place.

Just a few things I recall there. A friend my age, Mary, lived on the west side of the alley. One morning, she and I took an early walk down the alley, when we spied some of the prettiest tulips in a lady's yard. So we, being good little girls, decided to pick our mothers a bouquet. That night in the paper there was a report of a theft of flowers from a yard. We both lived a couple of days thinking the police would be there at any time. But they never came. I don't know if our moms called the woman or if it was just forgotten about.

When there was a parade or big event at the old Indiana University Stadium, they usually came down 10th Street. One day there was a lot of traffic in front of our house, and, child-like, I got too far out in the street. A car hit me, and I was thrown up on the hood. They carried me in the house. Old Doc Turner came. It seems like back then everyone was called "old" but everyone in Bloomington knew "Old Doc Turner." Anyway, he checked me over, and I was okay. Another time Mary and I were sitting along the curb when Dad was leaving, and he backed his car up before going forward. He ran over my ankle, and again, "Old Doc" came. Nothing broken, but for a week or a two, I had the prettiest little cane to walk with, which was the only thing I remember about that.

Next door was Billy Dixon's grocery. After I learned to sing my ABCs, I went to his store and sang them. When I got to "Now I've said my ABCs, tell me what you think of me," he would reward me with a sucker or maybe a little sack of candy. Surely, Mom limited my trips there.

THE CORNER HOUSE

Next came the famous "Corner House." This still sits on the corner of State Road 45 and Russell Road. People from way before my time had lived in this house, and I think some of Mom's family lived there before they purchased their home place, which later became our home place. We moved to the corner house from 10thh Street, but we moved a few times to Indianapolis during the weeks so Dad would be closer to work.

One of my first memories of trials was the rabbit test. My dad's cousins who lived on the farm where Marlin Hills is today raised different breeds of animals. They had chickens with feathers on their legs and several pets that were different. They gave me two white rabbits with big pink eyes; and they were mine. One Sunday, we drove in from church, and there were met by our dog carrying one of my rabbits in his mouth. He had gotten in the cage and killed both of them. I think that this is the only time in my life when I couldn't talk. I just screamed. And, of all things, by brothers laughed!!

There was a long porch on the south side of the house, where every night we got a wash pan of water and had to wash our feet, all of us using the same water usually, before we could go to bed. We didn't take a bath every day – just Saturday – but we couldn't go to bed with dirty feet. Our Saturday-night ritual of taking a bath was something else. We had a big galvanized wash-tub. Water was heated on the kitchen stove, and as the next in line took a bath, a little more warm water was added. We weren't ashamed of this, as this was the way most of our friends washed in their homes.

Down the hill behind the house was a pond. Many times we would run the hogs out and let the mud settle. Then we would get in and play in the water. The pond was full of frogs which we could hear all the way to the house sometimes, and this was sweet music when everything was quiet and dark. My brothers and whoever would go frog-hunting. Man, those were the best frog-legs you would ever want! One time they got so many, Gilbert and Ray took the sliding door off the barn and put the frogs on it to cut off their legs and skin them. After their legs were off, the frogs would still squirm and try to crawl. Poor things! What would the Animal Rights people do about that today? Not long before Mom died, one of her favorite foods in a seafood place was frog legs.

There was a hog lot beside the barn with a lot of trees whose branches were sometimes low to the ground. We kids would climb up, sit on a branch, and watch the hogs below. You know, kids will be kids, and sometimes we would see if we could pee down on a hog. We had to do something for fun!!

We sometimes snuck behind the barn and smoked corn silks. We had to have the silks that had turned black. I don't recall what we rolled them in. Not that I was so good, but most of the time I watched my brothers. Dad caught us one time, and he whipped the boys with a strap from a harness. There was a blanket hanging on the clothes line, and I stood under it and watched. I don't know why I was spared. But that was the extent of the smoking I ever did in my life.

During these years, Joe, Esther, and Bobby were born. We were always taken to Grandma Marlin's house when a new baby was born. Grandma's beds had feather ticks, which were the softest kind of mattress, and we just sank down in them. (Grandma Baugh's were straw ticks, which weren't as soft.) We would lie at night on those feathers and hear the greyhound buses and the few cars up and down the highway in front of the house. If we were still there during the day, we usually got to ride the pony, "Old Happy". (There's that "old" again.) On holidays when we were there, we had to take turns with our cousins and didn't get to ride as much. I still have one of the pony shoes that Old Happy wore. It's hanging in our kitchen.

We also got to ride horses in the summer over at Uncle John's when they were putting up hay. They hooked a chain around a bale of straw and put one of us on a horse, and we pulled hay or straw to the barn or haystack.

New additions to the family always made extra work for us older kids. At an early age, the boys went with Mom to pick berries in the summer or they tended the garden, among other things. I learned to bake and cook at an early age while they were doing their thing. There were cows to milk twice a day which led to churning butter and making cottage cheese, which, by the way, was better than any you can buy today. We often sat on the back porch to do the churning. We had ice boxes, where the ice man would see a card in our window that showed how many pounds of ice we needed. He would put the block of ice in the top of the ice box. We kept a pan under the box to catch the water; this would have to be emptied now and then. Woe to the one who let the pan run over! We did have a cellar beneath the house where we could keep some things cool.

THE MOVERS

As I said before, Dad moved us several times, I guess so he would be closer to his work since he was now getting some jobs in Indianapolis. It was quite a distance down the Old State Road 37 and took much longer to go that far. He always wanted to be home with his family at night if at all possible.

We moved to a rental house a little north of Indianapolis to a little burg called Nora, where there was not much more than a grocery store. Today there is a town called Nora there. The house was owned by a wealthy lady, Mrs. Carey, who lived down the road in a large house and had a big barn where she raised peacocks, both white and the pretty, colored ones. She hired Gilbert and Ray to help take care of them. We soon had a lot of peacock feathers at our house. Mom kept these bouquets of feathers for several years, moving them from place to place. She still had some in vases and put them on the pianos in our tabernacles years later. One of my fond memories at this house was waking up most morning before daylight and hearing Lula Bell and Scotty singing "Lamplighting Time in the Valley," which was their theme song on the radio. I don't know how long we lived there, but we always went back to

Bloomington on weekends, either to the corner house or now and then to visit one of the Grandmas.

The next place we landed was to a house on 33rd Street in Indianapolis. There were stories that this house was haunted, which made for a lot of excitement for us kids. One weekend, one of Dad's employees stayed at our house and slept downstairs on the couch. He said he saw some envelopes pass before his eyes in the night. Sometimes one of the family would say they heard papers rattle downstairs when they were in bed upstairs. Maybe one tale led to another. I don't believe in such things, but it kept a mystery going. There was a dark cubbyhole under a stairway where Gilbert and a cousin would sometimes lock me and scare me to death. No wonder I have claustrophobia yet today. One weekend, we came back from Bloomington to find our house turned upside down. Flour, sugar, milk, etc. covered the kitchen floor; toilet paper was strung from top to bottom; tomatoes were splattered against the walls, and everything else you could think of. Mom was pregnant with Don, and needless to say, she had to go to bed. The police were called, and four days later, they found that two girls, 12 and 13, from down the street had done all this damage. Cleaners were hired to clean up the mess.

The neighbors across the alley had three kids of about our ages. We were playing at their house one evening. I don't know what their mother said to me, but I told her she wasn't my boss and then went home and bragged about it. Dad took me to the bedroom and said I could either get a spanking or I could go over and apologize. So he let me print a note saying I was sorry, and I took it over to her. Dad often made us "eat crow" for punishment. Seems like my life centered on what Dad did or said. But, he usually didn't get mad but more or less tried to teach us. Mom had her hands full raising kids, and she just corrected us on the spur of the moment. She must have done a lot of sewing and mending, because when we crossed her, she pecked us on the head with her thimble. She always seemed to have that thimble handy when she wanted our attention. Maybe that is why some of us are so bull-headed; our heads got calloused.

We were getting ready to move again back home and told the teachers and students we wouldn't be back. But for three days, we showed up at school before we finally moved. Joe has always said those little girls cried for three days because he was leaving. None of us ever believed him.

Another of our moves was to a house on 42nd and Waghorst Streets in Indianapolis. I made friends with a girl who lived up the street from us and sometimes got to go there to play. Her family was Italian; they were the noisest people, but I thought they were the happiest people I had ever been around, even though I couldn't understand them sometimes.

That was the highlight of that move for me. One weekend, we left to go back to Indy, and our car was hit before we left Bloomington in front of Grandma Marlin's house. We had to wire the doors shut, and it was sure a wreck. I remember hoping none of my friends would see us driving in home in that old junkie car.

Later we moved to Bloomington on Fess Avenue. We walked to the McCalla School, which was almost a mile, but walking by blocks didn't seem that far. I had to wear long cotton socks, but when some of my friends and I got far enough away from home, we rolled our socks down for the day. At McCalla, we had music classes, where I learned a little about notes, etc. I realize now that God was preparing me to play the kind of music I was supposed to play in future years. At each school I went to that had a music class, I learned a little more. God didn't intend for me to be a concert pianist, or I would have taken lessons and maybe wouldn't have been used in the gospel and church music for most of my life. Prov. 30:15-16: The writer asks God not to give him too much or too little, but Just Enough. I believe this is true in every phase of life, whether money, poverty, talent, or whatever. God knows just what we need.

THE HOME PLACE

My Grandpa Baugh died in March 1932. Two years later, Grandma married Bertie Galyan. The home place had a mortgage and some bills due against the farm. These few years when we were moving here and there, Dad was negotiating with Mom's family and finally bought the home place to which we later moved. Also during these years, Don, Gladys Elaine, and Bobby were born. Mom and three of her sisters all had baby girls the same year.

This house had seven rooms, two bedrooms upstairs, and five rooms down. For a while, we didn't have indoor plumbing, electricity, and all those good things. The globes on the coal oil lamps had to be cleaned with newspaper when they got black, which happened three or four times per week. We pumped water from the cistern outside the back door. The cistern had to be cleaned out two or three times each year. Sometimes the men cleaning it would find a mouse or two dead in the bottom and maybe a snake, but we didn't know it when we were drinking the water and never got sick from it.

A boiler was set in the backyard over a fire to heat water for washing clothes. This was a back-breaking job – to scrub, wring, rinse, and wring again well enough to hang on the line.

Then came the wringer-type washing machine, but we had to turn the wringer by hand. With Mom having a baby constantly, it seemed, we sure had plenty of diapers along with all of the other laundry. Then we got electricity, and the washer was moved inside.

Next came the ironing. Wash 'n' wear hadn't been heard of, so most everything had to be starched and ironed. We brought the clothes in off the line when they were dry, and the starched pieces were sprinkled and rolled up, put in a bushel basket, which was always full, and then ironed after laying a short while. My brothers usually wore light pants to church, and these had to be ironed. Later we could buy pant stretchers, which were a big help. At first, we had irons that we sat on the stove to heat; then a handle fit over it, and we ironed until it cooled too much. We placed it back on the stove and got another one. Later we got gas irons that had to be pumped often to keep warm. Then came the electric irons, thank goodness. On Tuesday, I usually did the ironing and Esther did the house work and helped Mom. Sometimes it took more than one day. You would think with so many kids, Mom would not have been so particular with her laundry, but she was very much so.

One bad thing about not having a bathroom was at night; if one of the smaller kids had to go, one of us older ones had to take a flashlight and take them to the outhouse.

One night Mom told Esther to take Don. Someone came in the kitchen just as Esther told Don, "Cross your legs – it'll go back in." But she had to take him anyway. That old outhouse had cracks you could see through. Dad had a stud-horse, Old Tony, and always had bulls where neighbors brought cows to "visit." Sometimes we would watch through the cracks. I never learned about the birds and the bees; I learned about the horses and the cows.

As I said above, we gradually got electricity, water in the house, a bathroom, a telephone, and all those good things. Our telephone number was 9613. Again, isn't it odd what you sometimes remember?

When I was thirteen, my aunt had a baby, and the girl they hired to help with the work had left an opened can of tomato juice in the ice box instead of putting it in a glass ontainer. Bunny's husband was pretty much a health person, so he fired the girl. They had no one to stay and help, so Dad volunteered me. Back then, new mothers stayed in bed for ten days. I took care of the mother, baby, older sister, and all that needed to be done.

Oleo margarine didn't come already colored. It was a lump of white into which a package of yellow powder had to be mixed. One night at the supper table, I had mixed it as well as I could. But Uncle Slim got up, got a fork, and started mixing it better. I don't know why he didn't fire me. When I left there, he wanted to pay me, but Dad wouldn't let him. Dad said if I needed money, he would give it to me. To think I was only thirteen and didn't get paid. Maybe I got a little spending money from Dad now and then. Another lesson learned.

One of the delights of this place was that we could sleep out in the yard in the summertime. There were trees in our front yard, and we would take our pillows and blankets and sleep out there. We, of course, had no air conditioning, and sometimes it would get so hot inside that it was hard to sleep at night. Many nights, we lay right in the doorway to get what air we could. Outside, we were never afraid, although sometimes gypsies or a hobo from the railroad would come through. But we never locked our doors.

Our place was a gathering place for neighborhood kids or anyone around. We played in the barnyard and often played hide 'n' seek in the barn loft. There were a few stolen kisses sometimes. One time, a guy named Leonard was going to show me what a French kiss was. We were young, and I wonder if he even knew what that was. It didn't do anything for me, so maybe I still don't know, even today.

Dad had different ones working on the farm, and a few of them today would probably be called sex offenders. After the ground was plowed, a man would drive a tractor with a drag on it all across the field and back. Often some of us kids would ride on the drag. One time, the driver let me ride up on the tractor with him. I was probably six or seven. All the way back the field, he felt around the legs of my panties. I never told Dad.

I had an uncle who lived at our house at times. When he and I were the only ones in the house, I walked from room to room dodging his attempts to put his hands on me. I never told Dad.

One night a married farmhand was going to the store in Unionville, and Mom sent me to get some things. On the way back, he went past our house and drove on down to a church yard farther down the road. I would have been raped if I hadn't told him I was having my period. I never told Dad.

Just with a lot of girls today, I guess I thought I would be blamed.

While I'm on this subject, I can truthfully say, I never gave my body to anyone, except the two wonderful guys I loved and married.

PRACTICING CHURCH

We often played church at night. I don't know why because we went to church usually three times on Sunday and often two or three times beside that, but we liked to play. One night, Ray was the preacher. It seemed like he always preached on Jonah. We would yell, "Amen" or Yes, Brother." Then, at the altar call, we would all go forward to the couch and kneel down. Joe prayed, "Lord, I'm the meanest guy in this neighborhood." Immediately we all yelled, "Amen, that's right" and pounded him on the back. We agreed with him wholeheartedly.

On nights when Dad would get home early enough, we all had to retire to the living room, where he read from the Bible. We all knelt down while he prayed. If one of our friends was spending the night with us, they were expected to do the same. Sometimes we felt a little embarrassed that we would have to pray or have family devotions. But, oh, how thankful I am today that we did.

REAL CHURCH

Our place had an "old barn" and a "new barn." Dad had made a personal friend of E. Howard Cadle, who had the famous Cadle Tabernacle in Indianapolis which had a radio broadcast each morning for several years. Often Dad took a flatbed truck load of young people from New Unionville Church up to their services. He decided to make our new barn into a tabernacle with saw-dust floors, etc., patterned on a small scale on some of the tabernacles of those days. It was not nearly the size, and it lacked the grandeur of those famous ones. But it later was known around Monroe County, and at times it had a good attendance. We had different preachers and evangelists mostly on weekends but sometimes for a week revival. I was learning a little more about the piano and played for the services. This is where some of our family started singing some.

One minister came quite often on weekends and stayed at our house. Joe always had to share his bed with him. It seemed like every time he left, the next week Joe would get boils. A lot of people had boils or carbuncles back then, but we always said Joe got his from the preacher. One time, we went to the Stewart Tabernacle west of town, and they had "dinner on the ground," I had to take a pillow to sit on while eating because I had boils on my bottom and couldn't sit down. I guess antibiotics have taken care of a lot of things we "caught" back then. Another time, I went home with a friend overnight and got the "itch." I wore white cotton gloves with sulfur in them to school for several days.

A few years later, Dad bought a building on the corner of 15th and Lincoln, and it was known for several years as the Marlin Tabernacle. Many good speakers and singers were there from time to time. We had services on Sunday afternoons, so people could attend their own churches in the mornings. We usually went to the New Unionville Baptist Church for several years.

One evangelist came for a meeting. He was well known in revival work in Indiana as well as other states. I believe he had some Spanish blood, and I liked to hear him talk. His wife talked Mom into letting me go home with them to Indianapolis one night to stay a couple of days. The next day, she took me shopping and bought me a blue-and-white dotted purse with a reversible plastic cover. She also took me and got my first permanent. That was such a memorable occasion for a young girl from the country!

Years later, Dad let the Eastside Nazarene congregation in Bloomington meet in the tabernacle while they were organizing their church. Later, the Grace Baptist congregation did the same. The Marlin Tabernacle later was torn down, and apartments now stand where it was.

EARLY SCHOOL DAYS

In the early years, we were going to Poplar Grove School when we were living in the country. My teacher in the "little room" (this was a two-room school) let me take the second and third grades the same year. (I must have been smart back then.) When I got to the fifth grade, I got to go to the "big room." There, my teacher was Oscar Swindler who owned a grocery store on East 10th Street just west after going under the railroad bridge to Bloomington where today there are I.U. buildings. Each morning, he gave us time to say a poem, read a Bible verse, play the piano, or do anything we wanted to entertain the class. Sometimes Ray or one of the Arnold boys would play something by chord, using the hunt-and-peck system. And we always said the Pledge of Allegiance.

Every girl had an autograph book where others wrote little "sayings." For instance, here are a few from my book:

> ***"When you get married and have twins, don't come to me for safety pins."***
>
> ***"When you see a cat running up a tree, pull it's tail and think of me."***
>
> ***"Yours til the Plymouth Rock lays eggs."***

"Yours til the bobby pins get sick riding on permanent waves."

Back to the fifth grade. Rev. Roscoe Boston was holding a revival at our church. That one night, the house was full and extra chairs were added to the front of the church where some of we younger ones sat. My school teacher was there! At the invitation, I slipped off my chair right down to the altar – I didn't even have to walk. I went forward because I didn't want to go to Hell. The next day, I was a little timid with the teacher, but he was a Christian so I should not have felt that way. Since then, I learned that I am a Christian because God loves me, not just to keep out of Hell.

I was about eleven years old when, somehow, Dad managed to get me on the big stage at Cadle Tabernacle, where I played the big Baby Grand piano, while their organist played the organ for a few congregational songs. I am sure Dad was more impressed at the time than I was. But, I guess that was as far as I ever got to being a concert pianist.

There was a young lady who sang quite often in their services. One song she often sang was "The Sun Will Shine Again." Through my life, two lines of this song have come to me often. Troubles come and troubles go, and we often wonder when they are going, but ***"the sun will shine again, for just behind the clouds, the sun is shining. We can take off in an airplane and go through nothing but clouds, but when we get so high, there's the sun."***

BETHEL CHURCH

This little church on Bethel Lane had been the church where my Grandma Marlin had taught Sunday School; her children had gone there. While we were small, we attended there often. You can see we spent a lot of our lives going to church somewhere. Years later, Dad and Mom bought the church. He remodeled it some, putting kerosene lamps around the walls and electric-baseboard heat, but he still kept the old drum stove in the middle of the floor. I had the job of finding an old pump organ, which I found at a second-hand store for $75. It is still there. Several years later, our daughter and her husband, Connie and Dale Conard, bought it and today let different groups hold services there from time to time.

After graduating from the eighth grade, I was still twelve years old when I started at Bloomington High School. When I graduated four years later at age sixteen, I was the youngest in my class. Of course, this was due to taking second and third grades years before. I loved high school so much that I would have gone on Saturday if they had let me. Course, maybe some of this was because I would have gotten out of some work at home.

I took clarinet lessons the first semester, and here again I learned to read notes a little better. I made okay grades, but I didn't sign up for the second semester. I made mostly As and Bs except in Chemistry, which I didn't like. I especially liked Shorthand, and in my Senior year, I got to go to Muncie to a State Shorthand Competition in which we placed fourth. This sure helped me as I traveled with Dad taking dictation, etc. as he was looking over jobs. My Aunt Bessie was a professor of Latin at Purdue University, so I took Latin and really liked it. Years later, when Jack and I traveled to South America, Mexico, and so on, I used my Latin to figure out words and signs.

Two afternoons per week, the Dean of Girls had two or three girls come to her office before school was out to set up a table of candy bars to sell to students as they left for home. I was chosen as one of those girls one semester. Some evenings, the candy was so tantalizing. My brothers and I got 15¢ a day for our lunch, with which, at that time, we could go across the street to Lyons Drug Store and get a hamburger and a Pepsi. So, I usually didn't have anything left for candy. Now and then, I just had to have something sweet. I don't know if the devil made me do it or if I just did it, but a few times, a candy bar went unpaid for. Isn't it odd some of the things we remember? God has forgiven me, but I still think of it, and I think it helps me to understand others at times.

The seniors were having a play. Since I could never stay after school to try out for it, I did finally talk to Dad into letting me usher at it, but I didn't have a formal. My Aunt Mary had a long, lace dress that was straight up and down, and she let me borrow it. I was about 112 pounds, so I was a bean pole, while most of the girls had big full skirts on their dresses like Scarlet O'Hara. But I lived through it.

In the latter part of the 1920s and into 1930, a lot went on in our life on the farm. The Great Depression came to America, and most all families were sorely hit. People had to stand in long lines to get food and necessities. Due to the fact that we lived on the farm and raised most of our food and had animals for meat and milk, God had really blessed us, although we were not rich by any means. Again, as I quoted earlier, God knows what we need and when – ***Just Enough***. Even when I was a freshman in college, my Uncle Bernard picked me up one evening after school and took me to buy a pair of shoes, as I had cardboard in mine to cover the holes in the bottoms.

In the summer, the threshers moved from farm to farm to thresh the wheat, store the grain, etc. These men were made up of neighboring families who helped each other. There were usually eight or ten men to feed at noon. Mom usually had a hired girl to help us when it was our day to host the event. We did have an unusually large dining room and a big, long table. This room was what today is called a family room.

(One time, a nephew of Mom's who was an only child had stopped in while we were eating. He went home and told his mother that it looked like a picture of the Lord's Supper at our dining table).

When the threshers were there, of course we did not have an air-conditioner. With so much running in and out, and with it being summer time, we had a problem with flies. So while the men were eating, one of us kids would wave branches from a sassafras bush over the men or table to keep the flies away. Oh, we had a method for everything. After we got the dishes done and everything cleaned up, someone would hold the door open, and a couple would shake the branches and drive the flies out the door. We used a lot of fly spray, too.

During these years and the moves we made, Don, Gladys Elaine, and Keith had been born, which made nine children. I think it was 1936 when Dad told his mother they were going to have another baby and that he didn't know how they would feed more. Grandma quoted scripture to him–

"I have been young and now am old: yet have I not seen the righteous forsaken, nor his seed begging bread." Ps. 37:25

For years, Dad told that after his mother told him this, they decided they would just go ahead and have more.

That fall, I guess because the roads were not too good, we moved again to a house in town on East 11th Street just east of Walnut Street. Then, on January 22, 1937, off we went to Grandma's while Audrey was being born. Later, we moved back home.

During the next two years, life was getting busier and busier for those of us in our teen years. During our high-school years, we were kept busy in the summer with farm and household chores. Dad had started using my "smarts" to write letters, make invoices, etc. for his business. Thanks to a very good teacher, I was learning to use punctuation, spelling, and those things which have helped me through the years, but some of it slips away as we get older. I often went with him, and as he was looking over a job or was in a meeting, I would type the letters or bills that he had dictated to me on the way. We had a small, portable typewriter that we took with us in the car. I did this during my high-school days and even during the war at times. Two or three times, he took me to court hearings he had with different companies. I was getting experience with my shorthand and used it to note what was done at these meetings. If there was much to be done at home, I stayed to help Mom; otherwise, I was in school. At these times, much of this book work was done at night after Dad got home from work.

I had met Harold Rogers at church, and he also rode the

same school bus as we did. We became sweethearts, even though I couldn't date until I was 16. A lot of our "sparking" was on a bicycle – he on the bike and me standing beside it. Some nights, the Arnold boys and others would start out from our barnyard, some on bikes and some walking. As we walked, other kids would join us, and sometimes there would be two dozen of us as we walked to the Fleener School on Bethel Lane, which was about two miles. If I was lucky enough to get out before Dad got home, I went along, but if he had book work to do, he often came along and picked me up.

Dad gave me a choice of a wrist watch or a class ring when I graduated from high school. I took the watch. One night, when he had told me I couldn't go walking, I went anyway before he got home. He caught up with us at New Unionville and made me get in the car with him. He took my watch and kept it for two weeks. My brothers got to walk on.

Another time, we were having a cow sale. Everyone was busy with that, but I managed to ask Dad if I could go home with a cousin. He told me no. I went to the house and asked Mom if I could go, and she said yes, not knowing Dad had refused me. That night after the sale, he came to get me and took me home. For a whole week, he ignored me. He didn't answer if I asked him anything and didn't say anything to me. That was worse than any punishment he could have given me.

One of us was always learning to drive, so Joe and I were trying at the same time. One would get to drive to Unionville, and the other drove back. One Sunday evening, we did this, and one of us had a few pennies (which we probably found in the chair where Dad had sat), so we went into the store and bought some bubble gum. We went back home blowing bubbles – big time. Dad immediately wanted to know where we got it, because we were never allowed to buy anything on Sunday. We told him a girl who was early for the BYF meeting at church gave it to us. Of all times, Joe told the truth. Esther and I got a whipping with a belt. Esther never shed a tear, but I cried off and on for two days. I went to high school with a few bruises on my legs. It sure taught me never to lie.

After a time, Harold got a Model B Ford. Some nights, our dating consisted of Harold waiting while I wrote letters, etc., and then he and I got to go to town to mail them. And sometimes he got to bring me home from church. Some nights, Gilbert or Ray would drive the family home from church and then take his date home. One night, Gilbert let us out at home and left to take Doris home. Esther hid in the floorboard in the back of the car – unknown to anyone. I guess later when things got a little yucky in the front seat, Esther let it be known she was there. They sure took her home in a hurry.

In our early dating, sometimes if Harold and I were

sitting outside in the car, all at once he would say he had better go and would leave. I learned later that he was supposed to be home by a certain time. He knew the sound of his mother's car. When he heard that car come over the bridge about a fourth of a mile away, he knew it was her and took off for home before she could get to our house and make a scene.

The Lord gave and the
The Lord hath taken away
Blessed be the name of the Lord. *Job 1;21*

This year started out about like any other. Another baby was due in January, so for the first time, we did not have to be taken to one of the Grandmas'. Joyce Ann was born on the 22nd and was the first child Mom had in the hospital. I have been told that Dad called home and told us we had a new sister, and I told him we didn't want any more and hung up on him.

Work on the farm and household chores went on as usual. Some of us were in high school and some in grade school.

In June of 1939, Grandma Marlin died at the age of 74. If ever there was a saint, she was one. I heard my mother say many times that she never heard Grandma say a bad word about anyone. All her children's families usually went to her house for holidays or special occasions. She probably put up with our family more than any others, as I explained in discussing all of our moves.

Summer came and went, and we were back in school trying to date according to rules. And then we were out for Christmas. A few days after Christmas, Bobby, Joe, and Don went sled riding down the hill in front of our house. There wasn't much traffic back then on the road, but that day there was one car too many. Almost to the bottom of the hill, a man, who was living at the time in the Corner House, came down in his car, and it slid on the slick road, hitting the boys. We all ran down to the scene. I was a really skinny girl (not like today). But I guess God gave me what I needed to pick up Bobby, age 10, and carry him up the hill to the house. Joe and Don were scratched and injured, but Bobby had a ruptured spleen. In those days, the doctors thought a person could not live without a spleen. So, Bobby lay in bed for four days. The doctor told us not to give him water or anything. That was one of the hardest times I had faced to that point, as he begged for just a drop of water. He died on the last day of that year.

Little did we know, another tragedy would happen in May 1942. Three deaths in three years was a lot for Mom and Dad to face.

BOBBY

Robert Leslie was named for Dad, and the Leslie was for a contractor friend of Dad's in Indianapolis. Robert Leslie was born with a wen at the corner of his left eye brow; this was a small cyst under the skin about the size of a small marble. Today, this would have been removed, but they didn't do much of that kind of surgery then. It didn't affect his looks, as he was a little full-faced pretty boy. He was a little "Dutchy" in his speech. At Grandma's one time, he asked for a cookie, but Grandma misunderstood and said, "No, I don't have a ducky on the place." "Chicken-no-wee" was sycamore tree. He could never say my name, so I became "Lala," and even today, some of my siblings call me that.

We had a big family but there was, and still is, something precious about each one.

I graduated from Bloomington High School in 1940 at the age of 16. I was the youngest in that class. I started college at I.U. in September but didn't like it as well as high school. Very seldom could I stay after school to study or for extra things, as I was needed at home to help get the kids in bed and ready for the next day. One of the farm workers would pick me up after classes to take me home – no fancy car for this student. I made decent enough grades and enrolled for the second semester, but I finally persuaded Dad to let me quit about halfway through that semester.

By this time, another baby was on the way. Esther and I slept in the room just above our parents' room. There was just a register that opened to their room – no furnace pipes – so we were always growling when we heard noises down below. That particular winter, we had the baby bed upstairs in our room, and Ann slept up there, so we had to give her a bottle or change her or whatever she needed.

I wanted to get a job, but Dad didn't think I needed to. Finally, I went to work at Western Union, which I really liked, but after three weeks, I was needed at home. Later, at the first of the War, Dad got me a job at Freeman Air Field at Seymour, where he was working. Again, that lasted about three weeks, but I did get a paycheck. That was the extent of my working career. When Esther graduated from high school, she got to go work at Public Service and even got a room with a friend in town.

June was born in June 1940, and I graduated in April. Harold and I were getting to date more, and during the summer of 1941, he was getting impatient with our dating "system." I was tied down so much. Weeks were full of work, and weekends were constant church meetings. Again, there was another baby on the way. The doctor had told Mom not to do much work and stay in bed as much as possible. We had a hired girl to help, but we were always expected to do our usual part of the work.

So Harold and I started talking marriage – secretly. He turned 18 in September, and I became 18 in October. We finally talked our parents into letting us tie the knot. Both of our mothers had to go to the courthouse to sign papers. Mom was so big she could barely get up the steps. On Saturday night, November 1, his parents went with us to our pastor's house down in the country, and we got married. Such a honeymoon we had! We went to his parents' and stayed Saturday and Sunday nights. Nothing went on as I was not "in shape." Even though one guy who had wanted to date me told Dad he would find out in a few months why we got married so quickly, but it sure wasn't a shotgun wedding.

Early Monday morning, Harold left at about four o'clock and went with Dad to Peoria, Illinois to work all week. There again I had to stay home because the new baby, Gene, would be born that week, and Mom would need help for about two weeks even though they had hired Helen Fielder (Miller, Barrow) to help. She was my closest friend at that time and was for several years. I was needed for another week, so during that time, Harold found an apartment in Peoria up above a bakery, where we lived for about three weeks until the job there was done.

We moved to the famous Corner House, and he started working at Camp Atterbury. He would have to chop enough wood after supper to burn in our drum stove the next day. We used only two rooms, so we wouldn't have to heat the whole house.

Next, we got an apartment at Edinburgh. Even though it was in town, it still had an outside John. In the kitchen, there was a pitcher pump over a large sink where we got our water. But we were happy.

After all, we were children of the times when:

"We were before the pill, before the population explosion, air-conditioned cars and homes, Television, nylon, and Xerox. We didn't know what credit cards were; a chip meant a piece of wood; hardware meant hardware; and software was not even a word.

We were before ice-makers and dishwashers and even refrigerators, before Saran or Tupperware. We were before electric blankets, pantyhose, and drip-dry clothes.

That was before men wore long hair and earrings and women wore bikinis. We got married first and then lived together. Coke was something you drank and was bought for 5¢; and pot was something you cooked in."

While living at Edinburgh, I would get homesick for June, who was almost two, so Dad would bring her over as he went to the job, and I would keep her a day or two at a time. You would think I would have liked to get away from kids, but I think in big families, as a rule, everybody likes each other – at times.

TRAGEDY STRIKES AGAIN

World War II was happening fast, and people could not buy gasoline or sugar without stamps. One morning in May, Mom got up early and drove down to the school to sign up for gas and sugar stamps. She thought she would get back before the kids got up, but Gladys Elaine got up, went to the kitchen, and tried to put a stick of wood in the kitchen stove. She caught her dress on fire, and she immediately ran across the road to a neighbor's house. By the time she got there, all that was left of her dress was the collar. There were no burn centers like today, so she was treated at the Bloomington Hospital for about three weeks. before she died at age 8. Her bed had a canopy-like tent covered with flannel. I think I will always remember the smell of burnt flesh mingled with the flannel. Most of the time, she laid on her stomach in a liquid solution. The nurses and doctor would pull layers of black burned skin off her back with large tweezers. On the 31st of May, she died. As I stated before, there were three deaths in three years for our family.

No one had to have counselors come in or go to a psychologist. Back then, everybody helped each other, and most of all, we relied on the Lord. I remember for a short while,

Dad questioned if he had done something wrong, because he and Mom had gone to see The Ten Commandments at a theater. Going to a movie was a no-no for our family, but as Dad studied and prayed, he learned that the Lord doesn't work that way – to punish like that. If we as Christians do wrong, the Holy Spirit convicts us and God forgives. And often times, we do have to suffer the consequences, but God removes the guilt and helps us go on.

GLADYS ELAINE

Gladys Elaine was the sixth child to be born in our family. She was named for Gladys Boston, the wife of Rev. Roscoe Boston. They were good friends and often spiritual mentors. Mrs. Boston always had a smile for everyone. And as I look back on the short life of "our" Gladys, she was a really cheerful child with dark blonde hair and a pretty face. I don't know where the Elaine came from, but I liked it so well, I named one of my own Elaine.

When Gladys was taken to the hospital, blood was needed for a transfusion. When they asked me, I had to tell them I was expecting a baby. We hadn't told anyone about it yet, but it was no longer a secret. A few months later, we moved to an apartment on East 11th Street in Bloomington just east of Indiana Avenue. Almost every day, I walked four blocks up the street to a grocery to get a quart of chocolate milk. On December 2, 1942 (1 year, 1 month, and 1 day after we married), our baby girl, Connie Darlene, was born, and she weighed in at 9.5 pounds. Guess the chocolate milk had something to do with that weight. She was such a pretty baby – everyone said that, not just we parents.

World War II was under way, and Harold was drafted

and had to leave in February 1943. After he left, Connie and I lived sometimes at the Rogers' and sometimes at my folks'. Gene was just a year older than Connie, so they grew up together for a little while. I often felt Mom resented it when Dad would take me with him and Connie was left there, although Mom had a hired girl most of the time. Then, when we were at Mabel's, I felt like I was being judged at everything. While Harold was gone, my best friend, Helen, her sister, and sometimes others would go to town on Friday night and shop a little or sit in the car on the square in Bloomington and people-watch. That was the entertainment for a lot of people then. Harold's mother would write to him and tell him things that were untrue. He would write and tell me, but he didn't believe what she said. I was always under scrutiny. We were always taught not to do spite work, so I didn't have the guts to speak up. I have often thought that if I hadn't been so naïve or if it were today, I would have had the nerve to get an apartment just for Connie and I, but back then, young girls didn't have as much nerve as today.

Harold was stationed at Fort Harrison in Indianapolis for a while. Bill and Lucille (Barrow) Robertson lived in Indianapolis, so her sister, Dema, would take her little boy, Tommy, and I took Connie up and stayed over night now and then. They would watch Connie while I visited Harold. Then he was sent to Ashville, North Carolina. He left Bloomington with some guys he knew; on the way down, he got a rash, so they put him off in the hospital and then found out it was just from the wool blanket he had been issued. All the other men had gone on, so he had to make new friends.

I went two or three times to visit him. On one trip, I got on the train, and a black soldier sat down beside me. Soon, a white soldier got on; he must have thought I didn't want to sit by the black guy, so he asked him if he would move so "I can sit by my wife." Some time later, the train stopped at a small town in Virginia, and the white soldier got off. I have wondered since what the first guy thought when I didn't get off with "my husband."

When I got home a week later, I was so anxious to see Connie. I rushed in, and she looked at me and reached for her grandma. Boy did that hurt! But it sure tickled her grandma. It only took a minute or two for her to remember me and hold out her hands to me.

Harold was on maneuvers in Nashville, Tenn. He was in the Motor Pool where he worked on Jeeps and drove for a certain lieutenant. He met me at the train station one night when I went down to visit. The lieutenant let him borrow the Jeep. But since he didn't want to get stopped with a civilian in with him, he brought a soldier's hat which I had to put on. I pulled up my coat collar, and we drove to the room he had rented in a house there for the weekend.

We met another couple at that house who were from South Bend, Indiana. We became good friends. The woman's name was Norene, and she had a sister, Esther Ruth. I have a sister Esther Ruth, and they both graduated from high school that year. We stayed in touch, and later we took our sisters to Nashville for a graduation gift. While we were there at the Grand Ole Opry, the announcement was made that the War was over. What a celebration, but it was hard for me to celebrate. Norene and I corresponded for fifty years. She and Tom came to visit Jack and me after we were married, and we visited them a time or two in Florida.

Harold's closest friend in the Army was a soldier he met in North Carolina, and he was from Midland, Texas. After Harold was killed, Alex and I corresponded. His family invited Connie and me to come to Midland and visit even though Alex was not home yet. We rode to Oklahoma with a couple we knew from Unionville and then took the train down to Midland. They lived on a ranch and had Mexican farmhands who cooked their bread and meals out in the barnyard over a fire. Connie was about two at this time, and Alex's family sure made us feel welcome. Later, when Jack and I were married, we went to Texas and went by to visit them. After Alex got married, he and his wife came to Unionville and visited with us. Connie still keeps in touch with him by letter or phone. His wife has since died.

Harold was sent to Germany in May of 1944. He came home just before he was to ship out. The last time I saw him, he was going up the stairs at Indianapolis Train Station. As always, he winked and waved to me.

On Thanksgiving Day that year, our family was together at Mom and Dad's for dinner. Dad had just asked the blessing when someone knocked on the door. I went to the door, and a taxi driver asked me to sign for a telegram. I immediately opened it, and it said that Harold was Missing in Action in Germany. I sank down on the couch and started crying. I don't know anymore about the Thanksgiving dinner. Dad and I went over to the Rogers' to tell them the news.

For some time in the days ahead, I wrote to every government department and anyone I could think of, trying to get more information. But I could never get any further information. Some of my letters to him were returned with "hospitalized" stamped on them, and some were returned not stamped.

Friends and relatives were praying, and we just kept hoping. I had for a long time remembered the verse that says, ***"If I regard iniquity in my heart, the Lord will not hear me."*** Ps. 66:18

I wanted to be sure I didn't have anything to hinder my prayers, so I tried to do everything in my power to have a clean heart and a clear conscience. I wrote Mabel a letter and said I didn't know anything I had done against her, but if I had, I wanted her forgiveness. She never did acknowledge it. Harold's Dad was a genuine Christian and a very sweet person which he proved over and over.

In January, Connie and I were at the Rogers', and again a taxi driver came to the door and asked if I would sign for a telegram. I was so sure it was an answer to my prayers that I said, "Gladly," but when I opened it, it was to inform me that the government had declared Harold killed as of November 4, 1944. To this day, there has been no proof – they didn't find his body, where he is buried, or even if he was.

We still kept praying and hoping. In April, two of my friends, Helen and Nellie A., and I went to visit Helen's minister brother-in-law and her sister in Rosedale, Indiana. The second morning, we were sitting at the table, just talking and visiting when suddenly, God said to me, "Harold is gone." No, not out loud, but in my heart I knew it was the Holy Spirit telling me this. I didn't say anything but got up and went upstairs to get my breath. I firmly believe God stops us in our tracks sometimes as he has to me several times. I knew from that minute on that that was when Harold died.

Most churches then had a flag on their wall with a blue star for each serviceman from that church. If one got killed, they changed the blue star and put a gold one on. When I got to church that Sunday, I told the lady in charge of the flag that as far as I was concerned, she could change the blue star for a gold one. Well, Mabel threw one fit! She accused me of wanting to get rid of Harold, etc. I won't repeat all. From then on, I was really under a microscope.

As I prayed and wondered about the scripture I was depending on, it came to me that I was not the only one on the prayer line for Harold. And someone else maybe didn't know that iniquity in their heart would hinder prayers being answered. Later in life in many cases, God is planning something else for us, and we understand why we have to wait and let Him do the planning. I understand most of it today. The only thing I wonder is why his body could not have been brought home like a lot of other men and saved a lot of the mystery. But He Knows Best.

A NEW HOME

Dad and Mom gave me an acre of ground between the Home Place and the Corner House and helped me get a house built for me and Connie. For a long time, it was the only house along that stretch of road. With the building and decorating of the house, it helped my state of mind to go on living. This house lacked some amenities, like a bathroom, but it was a cute little house and some of my siblings were there often to help us in everything.

One day when I was going to Evansville with Dad to a job, we stopped on the north side of the Bloomington Courthouse to pick up an employee. He was a tall, skinny, black-haired guy named Jack Evans. That's the way he looked to me then. Later in the year, I saw him around the farm some. If there wasn't a need for construction, Dad put them to doing something on the farm. I guess if they passed that "test," he thought they were okay.

One night near the end of the year, Joe and Betty asked me to go for a ride. When I got in the car, I was put in the back seat with Jack, and we drove to Columbus. Joe and Jack had become good friends at work. When I got in, I smelled beer on Jack's breath. When he later asked me if I would date him sometime (I wasn't dating yet), I told him I would never go with anyone who drank. As far as I know that was the last time he ever drank. With Dad and my brothers "taking to him," we later started dating some. Ray had come back from the Pacific War; he and Jack became good friends, so we doubled with him and his girlfriends some. I had two other dates, one time each. I think they both thought that since I had been married I was "needy," so I didn't let either of them come back.

I had a 1940 Plymouth which Jack and I drove some while dating. Jack had a 1936 Ford which didn't have a heater. There wasn't much to do on Friday or Saturday nights (that I was allowed to do), but everyone would park on the square in Bloomington and people-watch. Some nights if it was cold, Jack lit a blow-torch and put it in the back floorboard to keep us warm, even though we had to crack the window a little. My Grandma Baugh used to say, "Poor people have poor ways," which was true. How else could we keep warm?

A NEW HUSBAND AND DADDY

We decided to get married on Dad's birthday, June 29, 1946 on a Saturday afternoon. It was a very hot day, and State Road 45 was being resurfaced with black-top. We were married in the new house and had the same minister, Rev. Hughes, who married me and Harold. Jack's mother, my mom and dad, and Connie were at the wedding. We would have no honeymoon, as Jack would have to go back to work on Monday. But that night, we went to the Roxy Theater to a movie, of all things! Isn't that romantic? But our marriage has lasted 60 years as of June 2006, so you don't have to have a wedding gown, honeymoon, and all that hoopla to have a good marriage (although I know it is wonderful for those who do). We have had many honeymoons since then, which I will talk about later.

I gained a wonderful little Christian mother-in-law and a family who seemed to be often concerned about other people. I guess that is where Jack got a lot of this, although I hope I have contributed in a small way.

During the next two or three years, we were finishing what was needed on our house. It took some work and planning with Jack leaving for work early and getting home after work late at times. He would draw water from our cistern and carry it to the basement before he left for work, so I could heat it on a kerosene stove and do the washing. Gradually, we got water, a bathroom, etc. in the house. For some time, he would go to the barn at the Corner House and milk a cow so we would have milk and butter. That just lasted part of a year, I think.

During this time, I had two miscarriages due to being anemic. Each time the doctor said we could try again, it didn't take much trying.

All the while, we were taking a lot of flack from Mable, my ex-mother-in-law. Connie was calling Jack "Daddy Jack," and when I let her go visit her grandparents, she was told that Jack was not her Daddy. What did a little three-year-old know about this situation? Even twelve years later while we were in Florida on a job, I was accused of spending Connie's Social Security money from the government on our other kids, which a lawyer proved different. I was criticized for letting Connie wear some of my sisters' hand-down clothes, which were often almost new.

Through the years, Dad kept saying, "Don't do spite work." When someone did us wrong, he often said to "kill them with kindness," which Jack and I tried to do. This proved true, I guess, as before she died, she said she thought of Jack as a son. When my mom died, she hugged me and said that she would be my mother.

On August 30, 1948, Sharon Elaine was born, weighing 8 pounds 12 ounces. Jack had been at the New Unionville Baptist Church where they were doing some work on the church. I had been there to watch and had crawled up the make-shift steps to the door. After we got home, I went into labor, and we took off for the hospital in a hurry as I had a pain that wouldn't quit. They didn't even have time to take my watch off. She was born within about an hour after we left home. What a head of black hair! The name, Sharon, was for my sister, Sharon June, and Elaine was for my young sister who had died, Gladys Elaine.

Eighteen months later, on March, 1950, Peggy Marlene was born, weighing 8 pounds 10 ounces – another pretty little girl. The license plates on the car had expired, and Jack worried all the way to the hospital that the cops would stop him, but we made it. It was the middle of the afternoon. Wayne and Howard, our friends, were helping pour sidewalks in front of our house. Peggy's hair was dark, too, but before long, it was turning lighter and we had a brunette and two blondes for several years. It's anyone's guess today.

The R. H. Marlin Construction work was gradually going in the direction of Indianapolis. So around 1947, the family moved to South Harding Street in Indy. The married children and their families moved up, too. Jack and I were the only ones who stayed in Bloomington. The younger kids had to change schools. Keith didn't want to change, so he stayed with us part of the year to go to Poplar Grove. When Ann wanted to finish eighth grade with her class at University School, she stayed with us that winter. I'm sure she was a help to us as a babysitter or whatever. I don't remember that having one more than we already had made any difference.

A few years later, they built a ten-room house high on the hill in Bloomington on some ground Dad had inherited from his Mother's estate.

Dad was involved in a lot of church work in Bloomington and started a Marlin Family Hymn Sing which met in some small church one Sunday a month. Later, this evolved into The Monroe County Hymn Sing, which supported a ministry to the sick, aged, and shut-ins. Gilbert, Ray, Joe, and Don sang as a quartet, and often, Audrey, Ann, June, and I sang. But we always had most of the families there. This kept us busy on weekends. Many times if a church was having a meeting and didn't have a pianist, Dad would volunteer my services.

One such time, an evangelist was preaching at the Little Bethel Church. I went to play for the services, and the preacher was having a healing ministry. He was to drive the Devil out of a woman and told us all to close our eyes, as the Devil would go into anyone who saw him come out. I was sitting on the piano bench and wanted to look so bad but was afraid to.

A well-known man in Monroe and Brown Counties, Rev. W. C. Chafin, was known as The Sunday-School Man. He organized Sunday schools and held Bible-school programs in the summer. I often went with him in the summer to play for a Bible school somewhere in Monroe and sometimes in Brown Counties.

Here again, I could never have done all the things I did had our families not been mingled together in activities.

With the construction business in Indianapolis where the eleven sons and sons-in laws worked and the Sunday routine of music, our families kept the road hot for several years. Babysitters were available when needed.

TRUE FRIENDS

I can't stress enough how everyone needs a close friend or a couple needs "bosom buddies" through life. I mentioned Helen Fielder (Miller-Barrow) earlier. She was my closest friend for all my earlier years. Then in our earlier marriage years, she and Wayne were our standbys. There were two or three couples who would get our families together on Saturday nights to eat and then play Rook, Dominoes, etc. Dema and Virgil Swafford and our family were often together. Church and circumstances often change through life, and this happened, but Helen always stayed a part of my birth family as she and I played for the Hymn Sings, which Dad fostered in Monroe County, and a lot of other occasions.

Later, we became very close with Jim and Mary Thompson. We took a lot of vacations together and formed a kinship that never quit. We tried to take our kids on a vacation together and then went by ourselves each year. One year, we took them to the Smokies. At one stop, I was a short ways from the car when I saw a bear coming up the trail. I ran and jumped over Brad, who was about three, and right into the car. Mary's daughter, Jill, has never let me forget that I was going to let the bear get Brad instead of me. Even now, forty years later, she asks me if I've seen a bear lately. A lot of our trips were to Nashville, Tennessee to the all-night gospel sings on the first Friday night of the month, and then we would stay over for the Grand Ole Opry. We have taken this trip with many other couples as well.

Rev. Keith and Sara Mann came to pastor at New Unionville Baptist Church in 1954. It didn't take long until they were our "bestest" friends, and this made us three couples for a lifetime. They were called to different churches to pastor, but we always stayed in close contact and visited back and forth. They finally moved to Texas to be near their children. We visited them there and attended Sara's funeral, but we did not get to Keith's. They sure loved our family, and our family loved them.

True friends are worth more than gold – especially those with a sense of humor and a sense of caring and with whom you can laugh and cry or just be yourself. This is the kind of person we now have as our true-blue friend for quite some time, Patty Perry. She is the most caring person I think I know. And we will treasure her for the rest of our lives.

Back to our little family. We now had three little girls to enjoy and take care of. God always prepares us for what we need. I had taken 4-H and had Home Ec in high school, so I had learned how to sew – not professionally, but well enough to make a lot of their clothes. Back then, a big fad was to make garments from printed feed sacks. This was nice material and everyone wore feed-sack clothes. But we did use other material such as Dotted Swiss which I made one time for Elaine and Peggy – one in pink and one in blue. I often dressed them alike except in different colors. Elaine always thought she wanted to be a cowgirl, so we had to dress her that way a lot. A few years later on one Mother's Day, we were going to church. That was when women wore hats and white gloves. Peggy just had to have some white gloves, so I gave her mine. She walked in the church as big as anyone with the fingers on her gloves hanging down below her fingertips.

Memories are made of such as this.

On Saturday nights, often Jack would stand a daughter in the kitchen sink and give them a bath, while I polished white shoes and even the laces in preparation for church the next day. We seldom ever missed church.

How different the way people dress for church today. Of course, God looks on the heart rather than the dress. Personally, I think we should ***"Give of our best to the Master."*** I realize times have changed, but God did give of His Best for us.

A lot of people today remember Connie in a little white fur coat and hat, which she often wore.

A lot of people today remember Connie in a little white fur coat and hat, which she often wore.

Something happened about this time that I can never forget. One night, Jack had gone to visit a family who had had a death. Back then, visitation was usually in the home. That night while Jack was gone, I had put the girls to bed upstairs, and they were asleep. All at once, I got this awful urge – a pulling at me to go upstairs and do something to the girls. It was strong. I started praying and walking the floor. I went outside on the porch for some air. Never before had I experienced this awful pull. I called Jack to come home. This finally passed, but I have often said that had I not known the Lord, I could be serving a life sentence. When I read about or see that someone has said the Lord told them to kill their children, I wonder if they had this awful drawing from the Devil and blamed it on the Lord. One time, I heard an elderly minister say that if you don't know Christ, you don't know what you might do in any situation. I never once thought it was the Lord drawing me to danger, and I knew: ***"Greater Is He that is in you, than he that is in the world."***

In 1952, we rented an apartment in Lafayette where Jack would be working for some time. We moved the necessary furniture in a dump truck. But we went home each weekend. I don't know why, but us Marlins thought we had to be in Bloomington each weekend. Just couldn't stay away.

Our landlords were caretakers for the zoo, which was about three blocks away. Sometimes, early in the morning, we could hear the lions roar. On one side of us was a family with two little boys. We just couldn't get over seeing the dad sitting outside giving the boys a drink of his beer now and then. Today, we would probably "turn him in."

Connie enrolled in fourth grade there. We bought her a bicycle which she rode, and she sometimes walked to school. The other two were not in school yet, so they had a tricycle to ride up and down the sidewalk. We got our first TV there. I started watching the soaps, Search for Tomorrow being about the first one. A few years later, I felt like our family was having enough soap episodes of our own, and I got weaned away.

We moved back around the first of August as I was expecting a baby. Again, my family came to our rescue: Audrey came to stay with me. The night I went into labor, she called Jack in Lafayette and then took me to the hospital, where he met us shortly after. I say shortly because he "speeded" home.

AUGUST 29, 1952

Randy Jack was born, weighing in at 8 pounds even. He was the smallest baby I had had but looked the biggest. The doctor said he would probably be a football player with the big shoulders he had. Jack drove back and forth from Lafayette until that job was done.

After nursing Randy a few months, I got a lump in my breast and had to have it removed and tested. Dr. Baxter had an airplane, and his pilot was waiting to take the tumor to Indianapolis for a biopsy. There was no laboratory in Bloomington for testing. The results came back as benign. Later, I had to have another one removed from the other side, and it was also benign. I had to put Randy on a bottle, but he ended up preferring the silky corner of his blanket to tickle his ear while sucking his thumb. He weaned himself from the bottle just before he was a year old, but he carried this blanket habit for a few years, which was sometimes a little embarrassing when he would pull his hair down to tickle his ear when he was sleepy.

When Elaine was about a month old, I took her and went down to the school and met with some other women, and we organized the Husmor Home Demonstration Club.

I was still a charter member when it disbanded. A year or two later, the Shamrock Home Demonstration Club was formed, and I joined it. I was very much involved in these two clubs for about twenty-five years. This included work at fair times and various activities. Jack and I tried to keep up with PTA, etc., along with the church, so we stayed busy.

In 1954, a job was coming up in Louisville, so we bought a house trailer and moved to Jeffersonville. We had four kids now and this was not a very big trailer. It had bunk beds along the aisle. We made the couch in the living room into a bed at night. The table was a corner table that had to be pulled out each time we ate. It had folding chairs that stored under the table. But somehow I think I kept things organized better than I do now.

Connie was in school at Jeffersonville. I took the other three with me to the laundry room there on wash days. I always look back at those days as happy ones. Again, as usual, we went back home on weekends. When the job ended, we moved the trailer and parked it beside our house. Joe and Betty lived in it for a while with Kathy and Georgann, which made another two to play with ours in the yard.

Jack next went to work in Kokomo; he stayed there during the week and came back on the weekends. We now had three girls in Poplar Grove School.

Something was always happening to make life worth

living. One Sunday as we sat down to eat after church with one or two of my siblings with us, somehow the middle of our table gave way, and all of the food slid to the center and down to the floor. As we all gasped and then started laughing, Keith picked up a glass of iced tea that had landed upright and drank it as if nothing happened. We sure had a time salvaging what was still edible.

Once when Ann and June were staying with our kids while we were gone, they decided they would fix a "real" meal since they were tired of snacks. They made fried chicken, mashed potatoes and gravy, etc. When they started to pour the gravy, the skillet handle was loose, and the gravy all went to the floor. They called the dog to lick it up. What he didn't get, they took the dish-rag and wiped up the floor. They turned around to squeeze out the rag and squeezed it into the potatoes. So, no mashed potatoes or gravy. But they all survived.

At Christmas time, we were still at our supper table when someone tapped on our window. We looked up to see Santa Claus looking in at us. We found out later it was our neighbor, Harold Weddle, but it sure made Santa real for our kids that year.

Memories are made of things like this.

MOORES PIKE & FLORIDA

After ten years, in 1956, we traded our house for one on Moores Pike which had four bedrooms. Connie was going to University High School. She had met Dale Conard, who lived just down the road from us. He was an only child whose parents were farmers, and he knew how to work. He was three years older than Connie.

About two years after we moved there, we found out five of our families were going to have to move to Port St. Joe, Florida on a job. So, like the Beverly Hillbillies, we loaded up trucks and moved.

One afternoon before we moved, I was ironing and wondering why Connie had not come home from school. She and Dale called and said they were in Illinois. The next day, they came to the house and informed us they had gone over to Illinois and had gotten married because they didn't want to be separated for a year while we were in Florida. The first thing Dale said was that it wasn't a "have-to" case. This was in the October before she would be 16 (in December). I thought my world had come to an end, but it was done and over with. And, there again, the Lord takes care of things. Their marriage, I believe, has been a good one.

So, we moved to Florida. Port St. Joe was a small town where they "rolled the sidewalks up" at about six o'clock, but it was an interesting time, regardless of the roaches and sand. Most of us lived out by the Gulf and went to sleep listening to the roaring of the waves.

On February 28, 1959, Bradley Scott was born, weighing 9 pounds 15 ounces. I had sat on the beach that afternoon and got my legs sunburned, which hurt almost as much as my pains. Jack and the doctor sat and visited until the nurse called. This was a more natural childbirth than any I had had. I was more aware of what was happening.

The kids went to school in Port St. Joe. They learned to say "Yes Ma'am" and "No Ma'am." Peggy wanted to know if Brad would talk "Southern-ish" since he was born there.

In September, Frankie was born to Dale and Connie back home. Brad became an uncle at seven months old. Brad and I boarded a train and went up to help Connie and Frankie. As I look back now, I just wonder how much help I really was. On the train, a black lady held Brad and entertained him when I went to the restroom. He didn't seem to mind. My sister, June, went to high school in Florida and met Owen Presnell; they later got married, and she moved him to Indianapolis.

We came back to our home on Moores Pike in time for school. A while after, a friend of mine who was in a club with me asked if I would like to work part time at the Day Funeral

Home, which she and her husband, Stephen, owned. I had known he and Gayle almost all my life. She was having some physical problems and needed help for a while. I went thinking I would work part time, but since they got really busy that first day, I ended up working full time for a few years. They called me their girl Friday since I did a little bit of everything. I did office work, fixed women's hair, drove the funeral car, and did whatever was needed that I could do. One of the first things I did was bring a mother and baby who had both died to the funeral home.

A day or two after I started, two young guys asked me if I would like a piece of watermelon. They took me into the embalming room and cut me a piece of melon. I think they were testing to see how much nerve I had. But after that, we joked with each other a lot.

After I had been there about two years, I had to have time off to have a hysterectomy. The day I came home from the hospital, there, all around my kitchen cabinets, were bouquets of left-over flowers from a funeral, some not too fresh. What a welcome home! Jack had to get rid of them, but I did appreciate the joke.

Mr. and Mrs. Campbell were going to England for ten days, and I stayed in their apartment in the end of the funeral home. That was before computers and all the communication equipment we have today, so if we got a call during the night,

I would call one of the men at their home and tell them to go pick up the body. I felt safe, as the dead could not harm me.

Life was never dull on Moores Pike. One day, Brad and his little neighbor, one of the Kent boys. decided to build a fire in the field behind our house. The fire department had to be called, and I think for a while they thought they would really get it from the firemen.

Another day, Brad was out playing, and we discovered that he had painted the hubcaps and a side panel of our car with black enamel paint. Again, Jack to the rescue!

The kids went through a round of mumps. Elaine had a reaction to the medicine and hallucinated. She saw scarves flying through the air, goats stepping on nails, etc. I think she still remembers this.

We took the family on a trip to Florida, but Randy gave up a trip to Florida and chose to stay with his friends, the Siscoe family, who had three boys with whom Randy liked to fish and camp. He always seemed to like to do his own thing. I think he has a daughter today who likes to do her own thing, too.

While we were still on Moores Pike, a relative of mine introduced us to the Gideon Ministry. We felt that the Lord wanted us in the work, so we became members and are still in it. Much of our future was given to the work of distributing Bibles in various places.

SCHOOL YEARS

During this time, we moved to and were having a house built in Park Ridge. Brad began going to kindergarten, and we had a lady stay with him in the late afternoon. Sometimes the food at school just didn't look right to him, and I would have to leave work to go get him. They had some fish one day that was white-looking, and he really got sick. For a long time, he wouldn't eat anything white, liked mashed potatoes or gravy. I didn't think he was happy staying with Mrs. Wilson, so I decided to quit working.

I was beginning to have to cope with one of the older ones skipping school now and then. Peggy and Randy were going to University School. Peggy and three or four girls became very close friends, and they are still today. But for some reason, they liked to skip school from time to time. Linda's mother and I often had to hunt them down or go to bat for them at school. Sometimes the Quarry Hole lured them. I learned that no one can keep track of their kids 24/7.

Elaine wanted to graduate with her class at BHS, so we got her a transfer and bought her a car to go to school.

One evening, Randy did not come home from school, which upset us quite a bit. We made phone calls, and Jack drove around, but no success. The next morning, he came dragging in. He and a friend had skipped school and decided to go camping. They walked down the railroad and ended up in an old building and had a hard time trying to keep from freezing. Jack was chewing him out and told him to apologize to me. This is one regret that I have always had. I wanted so much to put my arms around him and tell him I loved him, but I couldn't with his dad reprimanding him.

One day, Brad decided he would leave home, so he put some things in a pillowcase and took off down the street. When he was about a block away, he turned around and came back home.

With all these things cropping up, how could I keep on working? But… Memories are made of this.

We were getting more involved in Gideon work and church activities. When Jack and I were first married, people remarked how quiet he was. After being in the Gideons a short time, I think the Lord loosened his tongue, and he has talked ever since. Through these years, he spoke in churches when needed to give the Gideon message. Each Gideon camp holds a banquet for pastors in the area once each year, and speakers go to other camps often when they are needed. So, often on some weekends, we went out of town to these meetings. By now, our girls were old enough to stay with the boys.

I was teaching Sunday school and took a five-year Bible study which met once per week. I still went to quilting class each week. Missionary meetings were held once a month at night, and I held various offices in that. During these years in my life, I was elected as State Scholarship Chairman of the Indiana Baptist Women. A conference was held at Franklin College for four or five days in the summer, where women from many churches went for fellowship, fun, and more information about mission work. A few years, as an officer, I drove another lady and the missionary to various churches for their annual association meetings. Most of the time, I got to stay the entire week at the conference but a few times was called home for something or other. One time, Peggy had had a wreck, so I had to leave.

During the summer, our kids went to church camp, which they always looked forward to. I went as a chaperone at first, but when our kids got older, I thought it best to stay home so they could be free. They went to 4-H clubs and exhibited at the County Fair some. One year, Randy was chosen as Fair King.

Then there was Little League season. Most of the time, I took them to practice as Jack was not home in time, but we went to all the games possible.

The American Baptist Churches USA was establishing a new format. I was chosen as a delegate from our district to the first Board of the Convention in Valley Forge. For four years, I flew to Philadelphia to the General Board meetings once or twice a year and came back and reported to the churches in my district. One time, it was held in Atlantic City where the Miss American Pageant is held and another time at Green Lake, Wisconsin.

I have said all of that to say this. I look back now and wonder how we kept everything on a halfway-even keel. I was never a "nasty-nice" housekeeper, but I was a clean one and liked to keep things as orderly as possible. But I didn't have to wash on Monday, iron on Tuesday, and so on like most of my friends did because I did my work on the convenient day.

There was a sign in an Amish furniture store, which read, ***"Once upon a time, there was time."***

People are in such a rush today, we can't take time. Somehow back then, we managed to make time. And even then, we missed a lot of blessings and memories we could have had.

During these years, though, we did take time for picnics often on Sundays after church – often at Brown County Park or McCormacks Creek. Two or three of our families often got together for these. In the winter, we would go ice-skating on Ott Young's pond and do a lot of fun things.

BIG BUSY JACK

One person said many of our kids grow up without bonding or having a sense of responsibility. Quality time will not always be available. Kids grow up and leave. Loved ones die. Someone we always meant to reach out to moves away.

I hope our children can look back and know that we tried to raise them to enjoy life as well as have responsibility. I don't think we have done too badly when I see them today and see how they have persevered through a lot of hardships.

"Once upon a time, there was time."

It was about this time that I wrote my rendition of BBJ (Big Busy Jack):

A Week in the Life of BBJ (Not Big Bad John – Big Busy Jack)
(Imagine, if you will, the following on fast-speed TV)

Monday, 5AM: BBJ jumps up, showers, and dresses; gives wife a good-bye peck at 5:30, and he's off to work (at 7:30). 5:30 to 6: Comes home. BBJ and Wifie go to MCL for supper. Gobbles down food and then back home. BBJ goes to bathroom. R-r-r-ring. Jumps up and out of bathroom to answer phone. Back to bathroom. Dashes on cologne and combs hair. Off to Board meeting, full of life. Back at 10:30. Falls into bed.

Tuesday, up around 5 to usual morning routine. "I owe, I owe, so off to work I go" – to more phone calls, frustrations, and work-a-day aggravations. Home at 5:30 to 6, full of life. Rushes around, gathering necessary papers to preside at Gideon meeting tonight. (More pressure.) Back home at 9:30. Sits down to watch news. Z-z-z-z. Plum bushed. Wifie picks up crossword puzzle or crocheting. R-r-r-ring. BBJ answers phone. Hangs up phone. Wifie asks if she should take the pigs to market or butcher them at home – she'll never know Z-z-z-z asleep again. R-r-r-ring. Phone again. BBJ gets up and goes to bed.

Wednesday, same time, same ritual. Gives Wifie good-bye peck – his after-shave scent gets up Wifie's nose, and she's wide awake. She gets up to a long day – BBJ is off to Indy and other parts unknown. Home again. Wifie has supper ready (for a change). BBJ inhales food between phone calls. Freshens up and is off to church for an hour. BBJ has brought homework home. Spreads job plans out on table and works till 11PM between calls. Off to bed.

Thursday, up at crack of dawn. Rarin' to go to the office and "East side, West side, and all around the town." Back home in the evening. Swallows supper. Washes here and there – more cologne. Grabs Bible and off to jail. (More stress.) Home again to more Z-z-z-zs and more R-r-r-rings. Can't stay awake to watch funny twenty-minute program with Wifie. Off to bed. Phone rings twice, but BBJ finally gets to sleep again.

Friday, same old "six-and-seven" day-time serial. Back home at 6. Go out to eat (again). Back home. BBJ's energy all gone – no meeting tonight. Plops down in chair; Wifie again asks when he will fix the leaky faucet or the squeaky floor, but poor BBJ is gone into oblivion or is on the phone.

Saturday, up at 6AM to shower and shine. Full of vim, vigor, and vitality. Off to the Gideon breakfast. Goodie! BBJ takes Wifie for a ride today. Just happens to pass by a job or where there might be one. Rest of day, BBJ runs sweeper and takes trash in between naps; gets glimpses of ball game now and then.

Sunday, up at 6:30. Spruces up to speak at church 50 miles from home. Hurries back for lunch. Takes a little ride. Back home to Z-z-z-z. Kids come in; kids leave – Z-z-z-z. Back to church. Someday, somehow, someone will slow BBJ down, and he'll say, "Where have all the flowers gone? I haven't had time to smell the roses (or my wife)."

THROUGH THE YEARS

Through these years, we were gaining new in-laws, nieces and nephews, and another few grandchildren. All our families were growing, which made a large number. Dad never thought it was Christmas if we didn't stay all night on Christmas Eve. The last time we all stayed, there were sixty-four of us. But, my, what fun we had, even if we didn't get to sleep! This was in their house on the hill in Bloomington. They had traded the house on Harding Street for a farmhouse on Bluff Road and had two houses.

We had moved out to Unionville Road. The boys wanted to go to Unionville School so they could play basketball, and it was closer to church. Elaine had graduated from high school and had gone to work at Stonebelt School for the handicapped and retarded. She had a special knack for this work and over the years moved up to administration. She fell for Larry Strain, and they got married. After a year or two, and after Brian was born, they lived in one of the units at Stonebelt and oversaw five blind retarded children. I never knew how they managed, but they seemed to enjoy their work. Later, they built a log house and moved into it, but she continued to work at Stonebelt for several years. More about her later.

We bought Peggy a car to drive to University School so she could stay with her class. Jack could probably give a recital on the cars we have bought through the years: the make, year, color, what happened to each, for whom each were bought, etc. While living there, Randy got a new 1972 Cougar, which he later wrecked. Something was always happening to cars, but I think Jack enjoyed wheeling and dealing in cars (except for the money part). My department was painting, papering, and decorating the houses, but his was keeping everyone on wheels. I think Brad took a little after Jack in wanting to be a salesman. When someone came up with a get-rich deal in selling something, Jack usually tried it.

Audrey had given me a recipe that made about twenty pie crusts. I would often mix this up and make frozen pies, cobblers, or crusts and put them in the freezer downstairs. They came in handy for get-togethers, church dinners, and so on. Ann and June had gotten married, but they couldn't make pies yet. Audrey and I often gave them our frozen goods as gifts. I think they tried to make their friends think they had made them.

One afternoon, my neighbor across the road called from her work and asked me if I had given Brad permission to sell my pies. Brad and her son were going up and down the road selling my pies for 25¢. They had given her babysitter one to bake for their supper. For many years, Brad was known for his salesmanship. Even today, forty years later, sometimes someone mentions this to me.

One afternoon, Brad and his cousin, Matt, went back in the woods behind the house to play. When they returned, all we could see of them were their eyes. They had got down and wallowed in a pool of mud and every inch of them was mud. Jack to the rescue! He hosed them down well so they could take a shower.

Things such as this, again, make memories.

Peggy had graduated and was dating her high-school sweetheart, Roger Curry. They were married while we still lived there. They lived in town for a while, and later, our first granddaughter, Alica Lyn, was born, a big 10-pound girl. They later moved to Tennessee, where Roger went to law school at Vanderbilt. Later they moved to Boulder, Colorado. I sure missed that new granddaughter. More about them later.

One day, I was standing at the kitchen sink, when Someone told me to pray. The message was so strong that I went and knelt by the bed and told the Lord I didn't know for what or whom I was to pray. I tried to cover each of our kids in my prayers and a few close friends. About two hours later, Connie called and said the tractor had turned over on Dale, but he landed in a ditch and did not get hurt. Maybe my obedience and prayers kept Dale safe. I would like to hope so.

I have been laughed at a few times for minding God -

not ridiculed, it was more like they just laughed with me. We went to a sales meeting in Las Vegas one time (one of Jack's sales whims), and a dinner show was included in the ticket. When we got there and settled, out came topless dancers, some of whom didn't really have much to show. But I began to get uneasy, and I remarked that I was a Sunday school teacher and I didn't feel right watching them. Jack told me not to look. But I made him take me back to the motel. On top of that, we had to get a cab. My sister-in-law never let me forget that. I am not a prude and am not perfect by any means, but when I know the Lord is telling me something, I'd better obey.

When I look back, I think we started raising our family according to Dad's beliefs, which I am so thankful for. But as I studied the Bible and learned more, I realized that a lot of the "dos and don'ts" were manmade rules. We could never play ball on Sunday, read the newspaper, play any card games except for Old Maid, go to or see movies of any kind, etc. These restrictions never hurt any of us, I'm sure, but I believe we can be happy and be in God's will without being so narrow-minded. But it took me a little time to realize this.

Dad had bought 1100 acres in Florida not far from where Disney World was to be built. Only the Disney Pre-vue Center was there. Some of our families went at different times and stayed in the house there. He was in the process of selling the ranch and had gone down there. He came back, sick, and was put in the hospital. He died a few days later on July 10, 1970 at the age of 67. He and Mom had celebrated their 50th anniversary on June 17. What a shock his death was! Needless to say, the patriarch of our family was gone. But his life had been such an influence not only to our family but to many people.

We moved to a new house in Blue Ridge. It was the most elaborate house we had owned and had four levels. I remember Brad didn't want to move there because he was afraid his friends would think he was better than them. A short while after we were settled there, Randy had married Ann Hancock, but they divorced not too long after. About a year after that, Ann gave birth to Jason, Randy's son. He had to have an operation on his stomach before he was released from the hospital. Randy was out beginning to "sow his wild oats," and Ann did not have anywhere to take Jason. So, we put a baby bed up, brought Jason to our house, and nursed him back to health. Sometimes Ann was there, and sometimes not. But Jason has always been special to me. Later, Ann married Jerry, and he adopted Jason, which none of us knew was happening until it was done. Jerry has been a very good dad to Jason. He and Ann are still our friends, and Jason goes by the name of Fox. More about Randy later.

Keith and Sara had been called to pastor a small church

at Mr. Horeb near Mitchell, Indiana. A woman in their church was an artist and gave oil-painting lessons. Eva Skirvin, a very good friend of mine through the years, Sara, and I started taking painting lessons. Eva and I drove to Mitchell each Monday for about eight years. Jack and I became very fond of Hugh and Hazel (the teacher), and they were like parents to us. They had a house in Bradenton, Florida for the winters, and we visited them when we traveled there. One year, they weren't ready to go down, and they gave us the key to their house and told us to stay there instead of paying for a motel. They also said they wouldn't even let their children do that, so we knew we were the best of friends. They later moved there for good. I don't know where a lot of my paintings (probably near 100) are today. For a while, one of them hung in the Auditor's office in Bloomington.

One day, I was home alone, and the Lord very plainly said to go down to Keith and Sara's. It was so strong that I immediately got up to go when He said to take $50 with me. I got my checkbook and left. When I got there, Sara was sitting on the couch crying. I asked where Keith was, and she said he was over at the church praying. She said they had a bill of $48.52 that just had to be paid, and they didn't know how they could pay it. I never knew what the bill was for, but my $50 took care of it. Just think, God took Keith's prayer 35 miles away and sent me to answer it. I know there is a God who is concerned and cares about little things.

One evening in the fall of 1974, we got a call from a woman at Unionville who told us that Brad had been in a bad wreck just below her house at Danny Smith Park and the Emergency was on the way out. We jumped in the car and headed out that way, meeting the EMT on the way. We turned around and sped behind them to the hospital. I'll never forget that siren sound even today.

Brad and a friend had been at the IGA in New Unionville when a guy they knew had stopped on his way from work. They asked if he would let them drive his car to Old Unionville a few miles up the road, which he let them do. Coming back, Rick was driving too fast and lost control and went off the road, throwing Brad out of the car. Two girls were following them, drove in the drive, and ran over Brad. This was what the state police decided had happened. The police said Brad could not have been driving, but it was a year or so before Brad remembered some of the details and knew that Rick had been driving.

The first thing the deputy said to us at the hospital was that there were no alcohol or drugs involved. I hadn't even thought about that. The owner of the car had stopped on his way home and bought a carton of beer, but it was still in the car. We should always know facts before we spread gossip. The woman who called us for a long time told around that they were drinking.

It was hard enough going through what we were without having that accusation being made. That hurt.

When we got to the hospital, four or five doctors worked on Brad through the night and for days. From his waist down, he was mangled inside, and both legs were broken. His pelvic bone was broken, and his bladder had burst. They couldn't set his legs until some of this other was taken care of, so he was in traction for a few weeks. Then, when they got to his legs, he had pins put in them and was put in a body cast with his legs spread apart about two feet between his feet. He was in this for a year or so. I won't go into all the details, but they weren't sure he would live. We had to get him back and forth to the hospital several times, and the EMT people would turn him sideways and carry him through the garage door and into the ambulance.

I believe it was meant for us to move to this house in town because of the many trips we had to make back and forth to the hospital. We would sometimes leave at night thinking the sleeping pills would put Brad to sleep and just get home when he would call and want Jack to come sit with him till he went to sleep.

This was a trial for all of us, but love knows no limits. You find out how many friends you have. Brad's cousin, Kim, was in school in the South and experimented some with short-wave radio. He told us he requested prayer to many people over that, even in the islands. I could tell so many things about those two or three years, but our family knows about most of it. There were times when I just couldn't pray. Sometimes I would go in the restroom at the hospital and beat on the wall and ask God "Why, why?" Somehow, my sisters knew how we must feel, and June sent me a letter saying they were our praying legs when we couldn't pray. Oh, that meant so much!

Two or three of the doctors told us there was a Higher Power who was in Brad's recovery. One doctor said he would probably never be able to have children, but today he has two children and two of the cutest grandchildren. This was the hardest thing we have had to go through in our lives, but it proves again that God does hear and answer prayer.

More about Brad later.

BACK TO THE COUNTRY

We were getting the itch to go back to the country. Mom had twelve acres left of the home place on Russell Road, so we bought it and had a house built. The one in town sold, so we rented a townhouse in Park Square, stored some of our furniture, and lived there while our house was being built. In our new house, we had a lot of room and were getting more grandchildren, so we had "little company" quite a lot. When one or two siblings came, other cousins wanted to come.

Jack tried his luck at selling modular homes, so we sold Brad an acre and put a home on it. In time, Kacey and Jared were close and could run through the field if they wanted. We had Easter-egg hunts and lots of fun at Christmas here. We had bought a pop-up camper, and the grandkids and I slept out in it a time or two in the backyard.

After some years, as with everyone, we were getting older and didn't need all that ground to take care of, so we kept an acre and built a smaller home right next to Brad's.

I was called to Jury Duty on a federal case in Indianapolis. I went back and forth to the trial for about three weeks. It was a case of four people in one of the "pyramid get-rich deals," and they had cheated people out of their money.

One of the group was an elderly man in a wheelchair. I often wonder if he has served his time. I forgot the details. We were sequestered for two or three nights in a motel in Indy. This was an experience, but I still like to watch trials on TV. Those that are real, that is.

Jack still wanted to run a crane some after he was supposed to have retired, but he didn't have time to do that and keep the mowing done, so here we went again and moved to where we are now – a condo in Bloomington.

I won't go into detail much on each family, as only they know all the ups and downs they have had over the years in raising their family. I can only say how we tried to care and understand.

Connie and Dale have always been so capable, and I know they are the hardest-working couple I know. Even though Connie was only just barely sixteen when they married, I guess she had learned a lot growing up with her brothers and sisters and knew a lot about housekeeping. And Dale had been taught to work. Connie liked to get out and work on the farm with Dale a lot. I never have understood why she had to end up in a wheelchair, which has hindered her doing what she liked. I can't remember a time they were away from each other at night except when she was in the hospital.

I have always felt bad that we didn't have Frank, Don,

and Joe stay with us more like some of the other grandchildren, but those little guys were always helping with the chores, animals, etc. But of course we loved them and still do as much as any of them. I hope Dale doesn't think of me as the "mean old mother-in-law" but as Mother. God maybe had a plan when Connie and Dale ended up with Jake and Clint, because those boys are such a help to their grandparents, and I admire them so much when I see them pushing Connie's wheelchair. I always know Connie will call two or three times a week, and our conversations always last at least thirty minutes. I'm so glad it's by phone instead of e-mail. I can tell by her voice if she is down or needs to talk. We feel so good that they are taking the boys to church and that Connie and Dale have a relationship with the Lord.

Elaine had her ups and downs. I mentioned her and Larry had built a log home and moved to it. She still worked at Stone Belt for a long time. Brian was getting ready to graduate from high school, and Isaac was about five years old. Larry had gotten injured on a job and was having a lot of back trouble. One afternoon, the babysitter brought Isaac home and walked down the yard with him. There laid Larry wounded from a gunshot. We picked Elaine up at work and met the EMT at the hospital. To be brief, Larry had fallen on the gun and was near death. They kept him alive until the helicopter could take him to Indianapolis so that some of his organs could be donated. Jack, Elaine, and I left as they were putting him in the plane and got to the hospital as they had just taken him into the hospital in Indy. No speeding ticket, though. For a while, they called it a suicide, but the coroner later said that it was an accident. The hospital tried to charge Elaine $25,000 for the organ transplant, but Roger Curry was an attorney and changed that. I prayed a lot about Larry for a while, as I thought maybe we had failed him in some way. Really I believe the Lord convinced me that he is in Heaven, but he was a weak Christian. He often had put his arm around me and called me "Mom." And we loved him.

Elaine worked and raised her two boys for about ten years. I often picked Isaac and Randy's two boys up from the babysitters', and I really enjoyed those little guys. Today, Brian and Isaac are two of the best grandchildren or men that anyone could ask for.

Elaine met an outstanding man, Jack Prince, and they were married with her boys' blessings. Elaine and Jack are in Ireland today, giving their "all" to help organize a church there. I can't remember a time when she wasn't making her life count for something. And now she is a Biblical Counselor and, of all things, an ordained minister.

Peggy and Roger moved back from Boulder and moved to Jasper, Indiana, where Stephanie was born. She gained a lot of friends in her school there, and they are still close today.

Roger was an attorney and was one of the best I knew of. I saw him in action a few times. While they were in Jasper, I remember one time Alica asked her mother if she could go to church that night with one of her little Catholic friends. She said they were going to have Midnight Madness that night (Mass). Another time, I was so homesick for Alica and decided to call her. When she answered, she said, "Hi Grandma. I can't talk now, my friend is here, and I've got to go." What a let-down! I have used this little episode in talks I have given. This is the way we do God. He wants to talk to us, but we just don't have time.

Things developed that only Roger and Peggy know, and there was a divorce. I have always felt that Roger gave his family up because he loved them and that says a lot for him. We still care for him a lot, and they are still friends.

Then Peggy met Alan Dick and remarried. I can truthfully say that I don't know of any two who are more caring and concerned about other people than these two. People remark to me about how Peggy always seems to be bubbly. Alan has a daughter and two sons, and Peggy has two daughters. They seem to be one big family, and as far as I know, they all get along just fine. I am sure this is thanks to having good parents.

Alica and Jim have two little girls now, Lexie and Allie, and we just enjoy them so much. Stephanie did social work and went to college in England for two years. And now we are looking forward to Stephanie and John's big wedding.

Peggy got her LPN license several years ago and has used her nursing skills in all positions she has had. Alan is a teacher at Bloomington High School.

For quite some time after high school, Randy was trying to find his way. He was a good worker, but he just seemed to always pick the wrong kind of friends. He was very kind-hearted, and I think often that was part of his trouble. He wanted to help everyone, especially those who used him to get that help. Many times, he took the blame for someone he thought was a friend, but if that person was a friend, he wouldn't have let Randy take the blame. So many times, Randy never snitched on anyone.

He married Belinda, and they had Randy Joe and Dusty. I can still see them riding in the car with Randy; Dusty standing up in the middle of the front seat holding onto Randy's ear.

He and Belinda divorced when the boys were still small, and Randy got custody of them. He raised them for several years by himself, with some of our family's help. I would go over about every other week and clean, getting rid of a lot of things that had accumulated. We picked them up at the sitter's some and often went to their school functions.

Sometime later, he married Melinda, and they had our last two grandchildren – twin girls, Miranda and Moriah.

They have always been so special. Though twins, they are different. They are teenagers now.

I will not elaborate on the past several years after they were divorced, but Randy got custody of the girls. His boys were on their own by then.

Randy was injured in an accident while running an earth mover on a job and broke his back. Then a short time after, he was in an auto accident. Due to several attempts and a no-good attorney, I took over the job as his representative to get his disability. This took almost two years from the time he was injured. We had to go before a judge in Indianapolis to finally get the job done.

I know it looked like we were always helping Randy for some time, but I never knew of the others resenting us for it. Maybe they did and we didn't know it. In any family, I think you help the one who needs it most at the time.

I do thank God that Randy has turned his life back to the Lord and is going in the right direction. I hope his kids will do likewise some day.

After Brad was getting over his accident, he drove to school. He met Luann, and later we found out they were skipping school quite a bit and meeting at her dad's apartment. They probably didn't think we knew. That's the way so many school kids are, aren't they? When school ended that year, they got married. They moved to the modular home that Jack had built. Later they had a little dark-eyed girl, Kacey Ann. Here Brad was not supposed to be able to have children, but God knew more than the doctors. Kacey has grown up to be a special person and has two cute little ones of her own. Later Jared was born, and we got a lot of pleasure out of Kacey and Jared when they were little as they lived nearby. Kacey always liked to suck on lemons, no matter how sour.

Only Brad and Luann know what went wrong; they ended up in divorce but are still friends.

I am sure Brad had a lot of times of discouragement from the wreck, not only physically but emotionally, and it takes a long time to get over an accident as horrible as his was.

I pray for Brad a lot as he is on the road so much in his work. I know he prays, too, as he has told me he does. When he hears a cute little joke, he often calls me from his car to tell it to me. This makes me happy to think he thinks of me and knows I have a sense of humor.

He follows in his dad's footsteps in construction and is now a sales representative for a crane company in Indy.

I have said that Brad's accident was the worst thing we have had to face in all these years. The next worst was alcohol and drugs. I think alcohol is the worst drug there is because it usually comes before other drugs. If children only knew the heartaches they and their families will face, they would never start.

We have no daughters-in-law at this time, only ex-es, but I know there are always two sides to any situation and hope they will forgive me for anything I may have said or done. It's only natural for parents to try to defend their children, but we know that isn't always right. So many times, our big mouths get us in trouble, but I have always tried to stay friends with them and would help them any time.

On March 2, 1988, my mother went to the hospital with bronchitis, and while there, her heart failed and she passed away. As I grow older, I understand so much more about what she went through for several years without Dad. I don't know how I would make it without Jack, but I know the Lord makes a way as he did for her.

During a few years' time, Jack lost his father and mother, so our children have no grandparents. But it has been said many times that death is a part of living, So we need to prepare to die and then live again.

We have had both the oldest brothers, Gilbert and Ray, Gilbert's wife, Doris, Don's wife, Shirley, and Esther's husband, Bill, leave us in death, and we miss them.

In November 1997, I had to have quadruple bypass surgery. I found out again how precious family is. When I came home, I had the best little nurse – Kacey. She had been working at the hospital, so she knew something about taking care of a sick person. I just couldn't have gotten along without her.

Six weeks later in Dec., I had to have emergency surgery on my upper colon. Again Kacey was there. Another thing I believe was God-sent was that it seemed like every time I was getting depressed or having a bad time, Peggy would drop in, not even being called. And Alan often made chicken soup from scratch and brought it to us.

Through all of this, there was Jack. He has always been the best nurse. He knows how to do housework or anything else that's needed. Of course, I hear from my sisters sometimes how he waits on me hand and foot.

Oprah Winfrey had a contest for best letters about husbands once, which I entered. This is my letter, and I still feel this way about my best friend:

Mrs. Elsie Evans
5840 N. Russell Road
Bloomington, Indiana 47404

This big 200 lb six foot three inch hunk of man, who most of his life operated heavy equipment can be gentle as a lamb. And, most of the time his is.

I was a WWII widow and when Jack and I got married, he became father to my little four year old daughter, and has been the same Dad to her as to our four children born since then. We have twelve grand children and one great child.

Jack is a man of "many hats". He is a deacon in the Baptist Church and is respected by many people. He belongs to the Gideon's International, which is an organization of Christian business men who place Bibles in hotels, motels, hospitals etc. all over the world. These men give their time and pay their own expenses to support this work. One night each month, Jack goes to our local jail to talk to the men incarcerated there, telling them God loves them and that others care about them, too, especially the men of the Gideon Organization. Just recently, after Jack had shared with many of them, three inmates knelt down and wept and turned their lives over to the Lord. He does this in a quiet, calm way-not preaching to them or at them. Among other things, he is on the Board of the Stonebuilt Council for retarded citizens in our country.

Though he didn't finish high school, he is an estimator for construction company which requires reading blueprints and bidding on many large construction projects around Indianapolis and Indiana University and various places.

But, what makes him great are the simple things in life. He gets down on the floor and wrestles with his grandchildren, plays ball with them, attends their games and school functions, and is a real "Grandpa". He drives me to the door at church or restaurants or wherever and goes to part the car. If I say, "Let's eat out", he never complains. After our family or a group of guests leave our home he doesn't leave the clean-up for me to do alone. He runs the sweeper if needed, and helps get things back in order, even cleaning up the dishes sometimes. He can run the washing machine, too, in dire circumstances.

We have done extensive traveling, and he always looks after the older people in the group, if any, and goes out of this way to keep everyone happy. I have always been free to go when and where I wish. He doesn't complain if I take trips with my sisters or lady friends. When I get back, he usually has the house cleaned up and the laundry done.

We have faced a lot of the troubles and heartaches of other parents our age-death in the family, divorce, drugs, alcohol, etc. But I 'm sure, due to his showing love and patience and our faith in God, our children have overcome them without going to counselors or professional help. We are proud of our large family (126 in all) and try to do things together when possible.

Oh, this guy has his faults, and he is not perfect, but I bet he is as near to being perfect as any you can find. And, I love him!

Thanks for listening,

Elsie Evans

February 2, 1989

Mrs.Elsie Evans

3840 N. Russell Road

Bloomington, In. 47401

Dear Ms. Evans:

Thank you so much for entering your husband in the WRTV/Oprah Husband of the Year Contest. We had a tremendous response to the contest, over 600 letters. Our judges had a very tough decision to make, carefully reading each entry. I'm sorry your letter wasn't selected.

Because you took the time to write us, it really shows how much you love your husband. Your letter was a glowing tribute to the man in your life. Several women didn't tell their husbands they were entering him in the contest, therefore I'm returning your letter, so you may show your husband how much of a winner he is to you.

I urge you to watch Channel 6 News @ noon on Monday, February 13th to see the five Indiana semi-finalists in the contest. The winner will be announced then. Also, the national contest will be held on "The Oprah Winfrey Show' on Tuesday, February14, at 4:00PM on WRTV 6.

Watching these programs will reveal what the judges were looking for in an ideal husband. Please enter the contest again next year.

Thank you again for your interest. Keep watching.

Sincerely,

Kristin Staskowski, WRTV Promotion

OUR TRAVELS

As I relate our many travels, I don't want to get boring or get to boasting, but I feel so many of our trips have been allowed at times when we really needed a break. The Lord at times seemed to work things out right when we needed it.

Some of the most fun times I have had have been traveling with my sisters and some of our girlfriends in the RV. Ann could maneuver that thing as well as any man. A group of us took off on two- or three-day trips just anywhere. We often took Mom and whomever. A bunch of women can find more to laugh about than anyone. One time, we took our daughters to "My Old Kentucky Home." In the course of a conversation, I remarked that I didn't like the word "pregnant" from the pulpit. To my nieces that made me old-fashioned and to this day, when I come around they yell not to use the "p-word."

My sisters and I took a cruise to Alaska and a lot of other places, and we always had the best time.

Ray's daughter, Eunice, was a missionary in the Philippines for quite some time. She taught at a Christian college. One summer, she brought a choir of young people on a tour of the United States. Ann drove them around in the RV to different concerts. Eunice's mother, Dorothy, and I went along. I truly believe their singing was the most beautiful I have ever heard before or since. I hope they have that kind in Heaven. That summer was one of the highlights of my life.

For several years, Jennings and Patty Polley have been two more of our bosom buddies. They had an RV, too, and we traveled together. Patty and I went on a tour to Switzerland, Austria, Italy, etc. We took a gondola ride in Venice and did so many things. In Austria, we went to see the famous Lipizzan Stallion horses in their big coliseum. These white horses originated and were bred by Austrian Emperor Ferdinand II. Their aerial kicks and jumps were meant as battle maneuvers. The Emperor gave them to the Hermann Family in the sixteenth century, and this family has trained and ridden them for the Royal House of Hapsburg in Austria and still do now.

They have their winter training sessions in Myakka, Florida, not far from Bradenton. We usually go to watch them train at least once when we are in Florida.

Patty and I once got a book which listed directions to outlet stores across the eastern states. We drove through Ohio, even on side roads, to get to some of them. We drove on to the Outlet City of the World, Redding, Pennsylvania. We got a motel, and then did we have fun. I don't know that we bought so much, but what a time! We have taken other trips like this.

One year, we went to Australia with the Polleys. We had dinner in a family's home in New Zealand. Jack and Jennings went snorkeling in the Great Barrier Reefs. We learned there are sure some weird things down in the water.

We traveled with Don and Dona Collins to England, Ireland, Scotland, and in that area. Don was such a camerabug. He took a picture from every angle of every castle. I tried to tell him when he had seen one castle, he had seen them all, but he didn't think so. We also went to China, Japan, Singapore, Thailand, etc. Japan was the most expensive place. We rode the Bullet Train. They walked up the Wall of China – I waited on them at the bottom. We walked across the bridge over the River Kwai so famous from WWII. This whole trip was very interesting.

When we traveled when some of our children were still home, we were sometimes criticized for leaving the kids, but as I earlier explained, we always left them with family or someone we could trust. Usually, the ones who criticized were ones who left theirs with a babysitter every day and went to work to make more money. Of course, that is sometimes necessary. Just lately, I told June that my kids must not have been too bad, because I don't remember coming home to them telling me something terrible had happened. She agreed that they never had trouble with them.

Our first plane trip was to celebrate our 25th

anniversary. I said we didn't have a honeymoon, so I guess this was our first of many. I had never been on a plane. Peggy had flown some from Tennessee and told me that I should try it and might even like it. One this first trip, of all places, we would cross the Pacific. I remember thinking, "I can't get out and walk," so I endured it and guess what – I did like it! Mom, Esther, some of their friends, as well as three of our close couples went. What a time we had in Hawaii.

Reverend and Mrs. Hittle from the Clear Creek Christian Church often organized trips and went as tour guides. They really knew how to plan trips so that we would see the most important things when we got to our destination. They planned the Hawaii trip. Later, we went with them to the Holy Land. The World Convention of Christian Churches was in Mexico City, and they asked us to go with them. We took a side trip or two, one of them being to the Yucatan. A little boy there volunteered his services to show us where the cheapest places were to buy souvenirs. Of course, he expected a return. His sandals were ripped so Jack said he would take him and get him a pair of shoes, but the boy decided on an expensive pair of cowboy boots, which Jack bought.

I guess the highlight of these trips was to the Holy Land. Like the movie, "A funny thing happened on the way to ??" There was a bus of handicapped people who went about everywhere our bus did. A lot of our people were about the age we are now, so they weren't too quick on their feet. One little retired nurse from Bedford, about 4 feet 6 inches tall, went to the restroom on the plane. Jack did not know anyone was in the restroom since the occupancy sign was not showing. He gave the door a jerk and lifted the lady right off the stool; she was holding on to the door since her feet didn't touch the floor. The stewardess came in a hurry to the rescue.

Another day, Jack was wearing a black turtleneck sweater. He had been helping some of the ladies onto the plane. When I got on, the stewardess told me I could go back and sit with the "Father." She thought he was a priest!

Before we got to Jerusalem, we landed in Cyprus. Soldiers came in at both ends of the plane with guns, and we were told to get off the plane and into the terminal. They had to de-bug the plane. I never knew if it was insects or war bugs they were looking for.

We visited so many places and feel so fortunate, as we got to go some places Hittles had not yet been privileged to go. When we read the Bible now or see these places on TV, we can see them so much more clearly. This was the first time they had opened up the road to Damascus to tourism. We went down the street called Straight, home of Ananias and Sapphira, who lied to the Holy Spirit and then fell dead. We went to the home of Mary, Martha, and Lazarus and to his tomb where "Jesus wept."

We went to the Mount of Olives and to the All Saints Church, which is built over the Rock where Christ agonized before going to the Cross. There were Japanese, Norwegians, Americans, and many different nationalities visiting the Dome of the Rock. We all started singing, "I'll go with Him through the Garden" in all different languages but the same tune. You could sure feel the Spirit so thick in there. As we left, the guide asked us, "Did you touch the Rock?"

As we stood outside looking down over Jerusalem, I felt some of the heart of Jesus as He had looked over there and said, ***"Oh Jerusalem, how oft would I have gathered thy children together even as a hen gathereth her chickens under her wings, but ye would not!"***

I stood there and thought of the times I longed to take one of my children in my arms and keep them from a mistake or a hurt I knew they were headed for but had to keep my hands off. How often I thought, "If you would only listen," but just as my parents did to us and our children have to do with theirs, we had to let them make their own mistakes and then stand ready to lift them up when they fell.

We saw Golgotha, where the face of the skull was, and had Communion served in the Garden nearby. We walked the streets of Old Jerusalem and many other places. We really felt we could sing, ***"I walked today where Jesus walked and felt His Presence there."***

Most of our other travels were perhaps considered mission trips. Emerson Ward, a friend we had met long ago in the Gideons, had gone to Chile at one time and made a movie there using people off the streets as characters in it. It was Something Better than Soccer. It was in Spanish, but he dubbed it in Portuguese. He organized trips where he took several couples to South America, and two men would take a projector and the movie into churches, schools, prisons, and orphanages. The Army Brass invited them sometimes to show the movie to the soldiers. At the end of the movie, an invitation was given, and many people accepted Christ. Then, the men would connect them with a church that would follow up on them. We went on several of these trips in a lot of the countries of South America. We got acquainted with a young missionary family in Santiago, Chile that we have supported and kept in contact with for all these years. They have visited us here a time or two. When we first met, they had two boys and a little four-year-old girl to whom we became attached. Just this past month, we were invited to her wedding, but of course we couldn't go. But, my, doesn't time fly?

We stayed in some nice places, sometimes in homes, and sometimes in not-so-good places. On one trip we made, two of us couples were put in a motel right in the heart of San Diego. There was a riot outside on the street that night, and the police sprayed colored water on the rioters in order to tell who they were. One time, we were in an open-air market at dark, and the lights all over town went out. I was in the back of the market, and Jack had walked on. I just worked my way to where there were lights on from the cars out in front and ran into Jack. Some hoodlums had thrown bicycle chains over transformers.

Emerson usually had an off day where we could take a bus trip to see something of interest, such as the huge statue of Jesus standing on the hill of Rio.

We really feel that we have been blessed in getting to make these trips. No one will ever know how many lives have changed because of this movie or from someone just giving them a Bible. When we went to China, which was just a vacation, Jack lined his suitcase with bilingual Testaments. When we went through customs, I was sure they would take them from him, but they ushered him on through. So when we were out sightseeing, Jack would give someone a Bible and show them the English on one side and their language on the other. As we walked away, that person was often showing it to another person. In Brazil, this movie was shown to 30,000 people, and 3,000 decisions were made.

Our children may not get a big inheritance like some of their cousins, but I feel they have had a part in this mission work. We could have hoarded the money and saved some, but I feel they have been a part of changing lives.

To our family:

I hope you have enjoyed this account of my memories, and I am sure there are many mistakes. But I know I made a lot of mistakes over the years, and some things I would do differently if I had it to do over – so please overlook these.

We are deeply satisfied with the people you have become and couldn't love you more.

I hope we are allowed to live and enjoy all of you for a long time, but know that if God decides differently, we know where we are going.

To touch on something I read one time, when God gets ready for your dad, He will probably drop his big dragline down and take him up. I don't know what He will send for me.

Mom

A Final Word

My ancestors on my Dad's side came from the County Derry, Ireland, and some from Scotland. John Morrow Marlin came from Ireland to America in the early 1800s and settled in Illinois. He and his family helped build and establish the Old North Tower Church around Herald, Illinois, where the Marlins owned almost all the land.

One of his sons, Hugh Marlin, migrated to Indiana in 1845 and bought ground just north of Bloomington. One of his sons, John and his family later owned the land where at present is known as Marlin Hills. They farmed that ground for many years, and it was later sold for a housing development.

Another son, Joseph Marlin, owned a large acreage on the Old Highway 37. The Marlin School today occupies some of that ground. Joseph Marlin at one time invented and got a patent for a mole trap. One of Joseph's sons was Robert Hugh Marlin, my dad. He went only to the sixth grade in school, although he had three sisters who were school-teachers, one of whom was Professor of Latin at Purdue University. He married just before turning seventeen and started in the excavating and construction business with a team of horses. He worked on many of the Indiana University buildings and many others. He gradually got better and larger cranes and equipment and built the R. H. Marlin Construction Company. Dad and Mom had thirteen children, and for over fifty years, there were eleven sons and sons-in-laws in the business.

R. H. Marlin was the first person in Monroe County, Indiana to have a telephone in his car, according to an article in the local paper. He was very helpful to many people and was very much involved in church and community affairs.

The ancestors from my mother's family include some Cox, Baugh, Richardson, etc. and were natives of Brown and Monroe Counties. Mom's grandfather, Isaac Cox, owned property where Danny Smith Park is now on Unionville Road. That property was a large farm and had a brick factory on it at one time. I've been told that Mom's great-great-grandfather founded Nashville, Indiana and donated the land for the courthouse and jail there.

Mom's dad and mother, Mack and Sadie (Richardson) Baugh owned the 160-acre farm which ran along Highway 45 to Russell Road. This ran back Russell Road to Baugh Road. The northwest part of this acreage was called the "Back Forty."

My parents later bought this farm after my Grandpa Baugh died. This was our "home place" for several years. At present, a cabinet shop is there, and the big seven-room house has been torn down.

Mack Baugh had a lot to do in the early days with building and making the grade for the Russell Road. He also did some of this for the grade Down Polley Hill between Unionville and Dolan.

So, both Dad's family and Mom's family have been natives of Monroe County for many years. Both Dad's name and Mom's name are imprinted on two of the bricks in the sidewalk in front of the entrance to the Fountain Square Mall on the south side of the square in Bloomington, Indiana.

www.ingramcontent.com/pod-product-compliance
Ingram Content Group UK Ltd.
Pitfield, Milton Keynes, MK11 3LW, UK
UKHW041852190726
13854UKWH00002B/855